HOW TO PLAY
PAR
THREES

Peter Smith

Colour Library Books

CLB 3430
Published in 1994 by Colour Library Books
© 1993 Colour Library Books Ltd, Godalming, Surrey
All rights reserved
Printed and bound in Singapore by· Kim Hup Lee Printing Co. Pte. Ltd.
ISBN 1-85833-057-2

Contents

Peter Smith

Peter Smith has worked as a writer and marketing consultant for over twenty-five years. He has published books on travel, classical composers and the painter, Constable. He himself enjoys painting, primarily in oils. Widely travelled, he has worked as a journalist in the aviation and travel industries, and was the editor of travel magazines in both London and New York. Peter lives in Madrid, Spain.

Introduction

Every golf course has its par-3 holes – usually four of them – and they are ideal opportunities to improve our scores because, for once, we don't have to drive a couple of hundred yards down the fairway and then hit another long iron to the green.

On the majority of these short holes the average length is about 150 yards, which enables us to reach the green with a middle or short iron off the tee. This gives us more control over the direction of the shot than when using a wood. There are, however, times on the longer par-3s when a 3-, 4- or 5-wood is the best club to choose. There are even a few of these 'short' holes where you might need to use a driver, particularly in windy conditions.

There is, of course, an art to playing par-3s, and the canny player who can master it will pick up strokes on his or her opponents on these so-called 'easy' holes. Even with the handicap giving many of us an extra shot on some, at least, of the par-3 holes, enabling us to reach par with a four, far too often we turn in cards containing a five or worse when, with a little more care and forethought, we could be hitting net birdie threes or at least par fours.

To find out best how to play these 'easy' holes, I have travelled to some of the best courses in the world and had advice and guidance from some of the top teaching pros. Not everyone has the time or the opportunity to visit these courses and take lessons from such professionals and this book gives you the chance to share the tuition and guidance that I have been fortunate enough to receive. The advice is aimed at the average player who doesn't have the time to practise for six hours a day but who can't wait for the weekend to be out on the course. It also concentrates on making the game we play a little easier and takes into account the fact that not every shot we hit is perfect.

The advice and encouragement from these professionals, so freely given, has helped me enormously and I know it will help you too.

Pinehurst, North Carolina, USA

Rich Wainwright, Head Professional

6th hole, 212 yards

"One of the most difficult courses in the world from 50 yards out from the pin" was how one of America's leading golf magazines described Pinehurst's No. 2 course, a 7,020 yard Donald J Ross design.

Certainly the hole we were playing, the par-3 6th, is very testing, even with its quite modest stroke index rating of 15, Despite that it is the most difficult of the four par-3s on this course which are, unusually in the world of golf, I think, all rated as the easiest on the course, the others coming in at 16, 17 and 18! Only Turnberry, to my knowledge, is the same.

These figures should not deceive you, however, for this hole is a challenge to golfers of all abilities. The hole may look quite straightforward with a clear run in to the green, but actually hitting – and staying on – the green is something else.

The view from the tee is of a fairly flat, wide – for a par-3 – 'fairway' with a bunker that slightly comes out into the line from the right, just in front of the green, and then bunkers either side of the green. None of them are treacherous to a moderately good bunker player.

The distance from the back tee, which we chose to play, is 212 yards.

Now usually on a par-3, you need to hit the green on the tee-shot. Here, that is *not* the best course strategy, according to

Unusually for a par-3, the tee shot should not try to hit the green. The best shot would be a fairly low-running fade hit with either a long iron or a 3-wood.

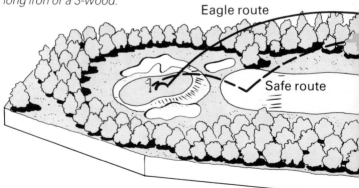

The view from the tee on the 6th at Pinehurst, designed by Donald J Ross. Bunkers protect either side of the green but none are very difficult to get out of.

Pinehurst

- **Hit long putts with the ball slightly forward of centre of the stance. This promotes top spin and gives better distance**

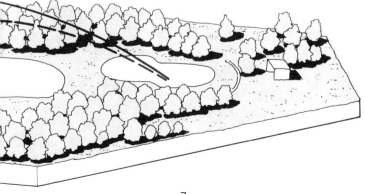

1 PINEHURST

Rich Wainwright, the Head Professional at the magnificent Pinehurst resort. Pinehurst is a complex of no less than seven golf courses, five of them starting from the main, large club house whose most important room is not the nineteenth hole but the ninety-first!

"Normally the wind is against you on this hole," he told me one afternoon when it was blowing a gale, "so you need to hit a low shot, one that is going to run.

"The average player's best choice would be a low, running shot aimed slightly left of centre with fade to come in round that first bunker. A 3- or 5-wood or a long iron should do that, although you have to be careful of the right-to-left slope immediately in front of the green. That will pull the ball across to the left, bringing that left-hand bunker into play.

"By going too far right, you tend to find the first bunker comes into the picture, and although it is not deep or too difficult to get out of, you would be faced with a fairly long bunker shot to a position on the green close to the pin."

The best shot, I could now see, was going to be a fairly low-running fade, hit off the tee with either a long iron or a 3-wood. Aiming at the bunker on the left, the ball should then come round as it approached the green. Exactly how far it would roll

Looking towards the green from a safe position. The pin has been placed almost at the peak of the green, so getting down in two is by no means easy.

onto the green depended very much on the strength of the shot, and of the headwind.

A careful player should have little real difficulty hitting to the safe position in front of the green, but then the problem is how to get down in two! With the index at fifteen many players will *not* be gaining a stroke on this hole, so it becomes a real par-3.

"The approach area in front of the green," said Rich, "is much deeper than most people realise from the tee. There really is quite a hill to climb to get to the pin if it is placed, as today, almost at the peak of the green."

This is where my long putting skill was really challenged. The green, as is common in the United States, was lightning fast. It was uphill so the putt needed to be judged perfectly. The wind also needed to be considered, as it can affect a putt more than most people realise.

I always find it helpful, on a long putt, to line up close to square, being only slightly open, and to take the putter back some distance to swing through with some force, extending the follow-through with the putter coming up pointing to the target. Several professionals have explained the importance of releasing the club on a full shot. Here, however, there is *no* release of the club, the left hand finishing pointing at the target, the right hand staying down under the left, the left wrist firmly locked, holding the left arm straight on the follow-through.

A good tip, that I have had from many professionals, is to hit the long putts with the ball forward of centre of the stance. The putter head comes into the ball slightly on the upswing, putting top-spin on the ball and keeping it rolling longer.

Pinehurst was designed by the legendary Donald J Ross, a Scot who came to the United States at the end of the last century and was responsible for some of the best golf course design ever. It was in 1901 that James Walker Tufts, the Boston businessman who had bought the 5,800 acres of timberland, for just one dollar an acre, hired Ross to design the first course, working with the overall landscaper, Frederick Law Olmsted, who was responsible for laying out New York's Central Park.

Donald Ross stayed at Pinehurst until his death in 1948. His cunning designs live on, however, and this course has hosted many international and national tournaments, among them the 1951 Ryder Cup. Apart from the beauty of this hole, and the course, visitors here can overdose on golf, with another six courses to baffle them. The PGA World Golf Hall of Fame also stands in the grounds, an impressive, living museum of the history of golf and its greatest characters. The top class Pinehurst Hotel is just a short walk from the clubhouse. And if the golf gets too hard, there's always the ninety-first hole!

*The long putt. Line up close to square and only slightly open.
Have the ball slightly forward of centre in the stance. Take the
putter back some distance and swing through with some
force, extending the follow-through.*

Krefeld, Germany
Nick Brunyard, Professional

13th hole, 148 yards

"If you have a handicap where, on a par-3 you gain a stroke, would you be happy if we marked down a 'four' on the card and moved on to the next hole?"

The question came from Nick Brunyard, professional at the Krefeld Golf Club in Germany, not far from where the Rhine runs down on its way to the North Sea in Holland.

Well, what would you answer?

Most of us, I am certain, would refuse the offer of a certain 'net par' and attempt to get down in three, lured on by a net birdie opportunity.

"Yet par-3s are often the most difficult to score on," continued Nick, "and I wonder how many players regularly par the shorter holes on their own course?

"There is, however, a way to play par-3s, particularly those where you do receive a stroke and where you are under no pressure to hit the green off the tee. Here, for instance, we have

Looking towards the green from the tee on the 13th. If you miss the green left or are long, there is a difficult chip back up a slope. Miss it short and you are in sand.

a wide area in front of the green where you can safely lay-up before chipping onto the green.''

The 'here' in question was the 13th hole on this excellent parkland course which, in 1990, celebrated its sixtieth anniversary, and is good enough to have hosted the German Open and countless amateur and European junior events.

With a stroke index of eighteen, many golfers have to hit the green on this hole, though that lay-up is still an option if you want to be certain of a four. Missing the green can leave you in all sorts of difficulties. Miss it left or long and you have a nasty chip back up a slope: miss it short and you are in sand; right is the only side where you have a chance of chipping close.

''The best way to play a difficult par-3 is really as *two easy par-2s*,'' Nick continued.

''Look for a safe position short of the green and 'plant' a flag there in your mind, then hit a short, easy shot at it. From there aim at the real flag with another short, easy shot.

''But if you are going to be short, *be* short! Not by half a yard or two yards; if you have room be 20 yards short.''

A hole like the 13th at Krefeld emphasizes how important it is that we choose the correct side of the tee. Going to the left of the tee cuts out half the green because a line of bushes impedes from the left. Teeing on the right is best because you can see the entire green. Yet it is amazing how many people tee up left and immediately put themselves at a disadvantage.

It is best to tee to the right here so you can see all of the green. A high 5-iron to the green needs to be hit accurately so laying up with a 9-iron or a wedge is a sensible choice.

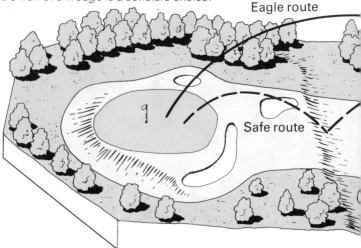

Eagle route

Safe route

Krefeld

- The best way to play a difficult par-3 is as two easy par- 2s
- Think carefully about which side of the tee is best to choose

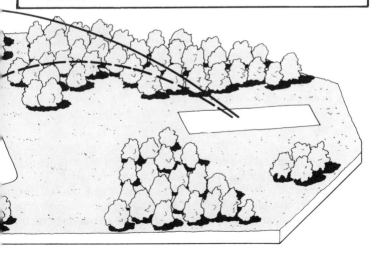

Running the ball up to the pin from a bunker with a 9-iron. It is important to have the correct club-release procedure. (Top) This is incorrect. The back of the left hand is still facing upwards after it has hit the ball and there is no follow-through. (Bottom) The correct way is for the left hand to turn after impact to ensure the correct follow-through. Be sure not to quit on the shot halfway.

"To lay up here hit a 9-iron or a wedge," Nick suggested. "You are then left with a sand-wedge onto the green."

If you receive a stroke, that is the easy way to play it. If not, and you feel confident about hitting to the green a 5-iron, the 137 metres (148 yards) to the centre of the green needs to be hit with draw coming in from the right. And that shot must be high and accurate enough to land softly, because if you run through – which is highly likely with a draw – you end up in difficulty back left of the green.

"If you are going for the green, aim for the top of the flag. You will then have a chance of carrying the bunker across the front of the green.

"Don't lose your concentration if you land in a bunker," advised Nick. "You won't necessarily have hit a *bad* shot *into* the bunker. In fact, don't ever think that. You have hit a shot into the bunker and now you have to hit a shot out of it. Be positive. Don't get into a bunker thinking you have to *recover* a shot. You can never recover a shot; it has gone. All you can do is to hit a good shot next time. Every shot is an opportunity to hit a good one, no matter where you are. It might just be to get you back in play, but hit it well (not necessarily long), getting the ball where you want it and you will then have played a *good* shot."

We hit a few shots to the lay-up position and a couple deliberately to the bunker on the right side of the green. This position leaves a 25 metre run-up to the flag, a bunker shot that Nick was happy to demonstrate.

"Use a 9-iron here as you have nothing to carry and just want to run the ball up -- the bunker face is low and you can just chip and run rather than lofting one out. Line up square, grip down, have the ball back in your stance and just take a little quarter swing. Let your left hand guide and control the shot. Make sure the hands roll as you come through impact, hitting a gentle but complete stroke, not quitting halfway through."

Sure enough, the ball just pops out every time and runs up to the pin.

Nick had some more interesting tips on winning golf.

"When you are on the tee, always look for some guidance on the ground to line up your shot, getting your feet and the club-face correctly aligned to your target. You will see professionals doing this, but make sure that what you are lining up with is not far away. I always look for something within a couple of yards at the most.

"Also, when you are practising, act as you would on the course. Line up every shot, going through a set pre-shot routine. Don't just stand there and drag balls towards you from a pile two feet away. Have them nine feet away so you have to move to get each ball; then line the shot up properly. This gets you into the habit of regularly checking your line-up and ensures that you are putting the ball where you are aiming it.

"A good practice routine is to hit three different clubs – say 5-, 6- and 7-irons to the same distance, about 140 yards. Use

each club, putting a different weight shot in to get the feel of how strong to hit. Get to know the 'feel' on your clubs.''

With elevated greens, or tees, there is also a difference in the strength of shot, or the club selection.

''To an elevated green you are hitting up, so your normal trajectory will fall short of the green; you need more club. To a lower green the opposite happens so you need less club.

''Finally,'' Nick concluded, ''don't try to drastically change what you have – just improve it. If you slice, use it, work on it. Don't totally change your swing, just improve it, be more confident in it, more consistent with it.''

Improved consistency is, after all, what we are all aiming for.

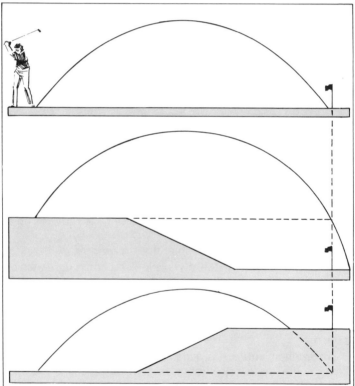

Hitting from elevated tees and to elevated greens requires either a difference in the strength of shot or in club selection. (Top) The trajectory of a normal shot. (Centre) A shot to a lower green requires less club or you will over-hit. (Bottom) On the other hand with an elevated green your normal trajectory will fall short so you will need more club.

County Louth, Baltray, Republic of Ireland
Paddy McGuirk, Club Professional

7th hole, 163 yards

Not far from Drogheda, in the Republic of Ireland, the river Boyne widens out as it reaches the Irish Sea. The river estuary is marshy and flat, with many sand dunes. On the peninsula close to the river mouth is the County Louth golf club, one of the hidden gems of Irish golf – off the beaten track and one of the most testing examples of a links course.

The professional, Paddy McGuirk, says proudly that there is not one weak hole on the entire course. Its four par-3s are regarded as the most difficult set to be found on one course.

The four par-3s each face a different direction so whatever the vagaries of the wind on the day you play it, you can be certain of playing one into the wind, one with it and two with a side-wind – unless it changes while you are playing, of course.

The par-3 that Paddy McGuirk chose was the most testing, the 163 yard 7th, a hole whose difficulty is reflected by its index

County Louth is one of Ireland's outstanding links courses. Its four par-3s are all difficult. This is the view looking back from the green towards the tee on the 7th hole.

rating of five. It runs south-west, so is very often into the wind, and, in the afternoon, into the setting sun.

Paddy McGuirk discussed the best strategy for the hole as we stood on the tee.

"The green is elevated, with a fairly long slope leading up to it, but the front of the green is protected by two bunkers. On the right there are mounds before you drop over onto the next fairway. Go too long here and you will end up down a dip that is far more difficult to get out of than it looks."

We watched several players hit over the green and take more shots than they expected getting down. The problem is partly the sloping green, which, if you have gone too long, will be sloping away from you. It is very difficult to stop the ball as you chip back up from that dip.

"Missing the hole to the left, or short, leaves you an option, perhaps the only one if you have failed to reach the green, because you can chip up from there. With the green sloping towards you, there is a chance of stopping the ball below the hole for a putt for four."

That, of course, is a net par but the lure of going for a three is not easy for we average golfers to resist.

The two bunkers guarding the front of the green – the one to the right is hardly visible from the tee – dictate that the best

The best shot to the green is high and straight with just a little draw. If you hit to the left, the sloping green helps to stop a chip, so a four is possible.

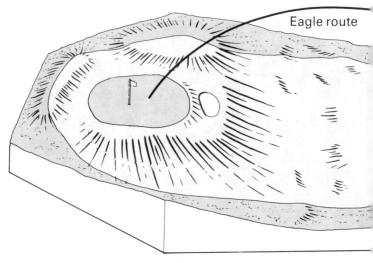

Eagle route

Looking towards the elevated green from the tee. If you go too long to the right, you will end up in a dip that is difficult to get out of. The sloping green adds to the challenge.

shot into the green is high and straight, with a hint of draw. The shape of the green means that a ball coming in with draw has more room. If it does keep rolling there is a bank directly behind the green to stop it – the ball might even roll back down onto the green. A fade here could put the ball into that dip.

County Louth

- **Improve your weak shots and everything else becomes easy**
- **If you slice from the tee, check the height of your peg. It may be too low**

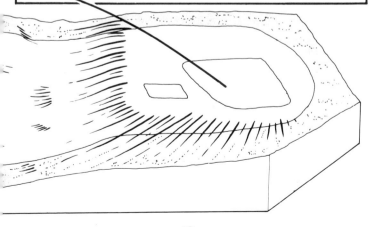

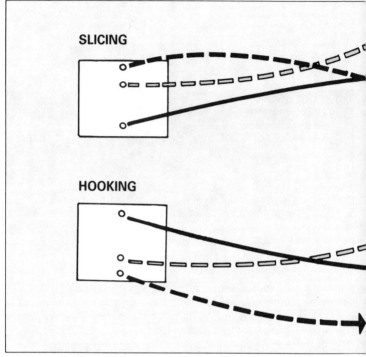

SLICING

HOOKING

(Top) If you slice, tee to the right and aim to the left, giving the ball the space to move round in. Teeing left puts you in instant trouble. If you find yourself slicing on the course, don't fight it but utilise it. (Below) On the other hand if you hook, tee left and work the ball in from the right. Teeing right puts you into trouble.

"Many golfers do slice," said Paddy, and the reason is often quite simple.

"It is the height of the tee that is sometimes to blame. A slicer often tees the ball too low; someone who pulls, or hooks the ball left often tees too high.

"But if you find yourself slicing on the course, use the slice to your advantage. Don't fight it, utilise it and aim left accordingly. The place to tackle the slice is on the practice ground. There you should be aiming to play the shots that you really dread when you are out on the course. For example, try hitting straight down a line of trees, keeping the ball in really close. Or hitting out of rough, or bunkers. Wherever you feel you are weakest, those are the shots to work on.

"Improve your weak shots and everything else becomes easy. It is a matter of confidence. Golf is played in a very small

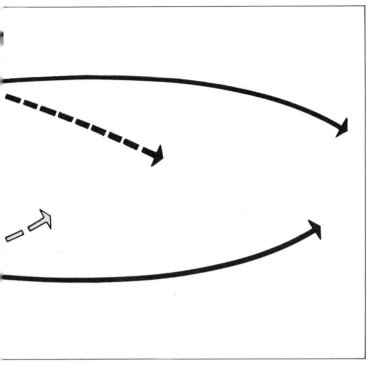

distance. It is not played over 7,000 yards but over six inches – the six inches between the ears!"

Using our mind does, of course, need to be tempered with knowledge of technique and strategy, and one of the most common failings is the way we tee, particularly on holes that have trouble spots.

The illustrations show just how difficult it is to reach the target safely if you slice and tee left. A slicer should tee right and use the full width of the fairway. A hooker, on the other hand, should tee left and work the ball round, with less margin of error.

These little hints are so simple, and so easy to remember, that it really is amazing how often we put ourselves at a disadvantage even before we hit the tee shot. A little more thought *before* we hit the shot would save us from unnecessarily playing *more* shots.

"It is a matter of confidence," Paddy reminds us. "Ask anyone to walk along a plank of wood on the floor and they can do it without any problem. Then put that piece of wood ten feet up in the air and it is a different proposition altogether."

It is, as he says, "all between the ears!"

Ferndown, Dorset, UK
Doug Sewell, Club Professional

5th hole, 208 yards

In the summer of 1914 the fairways at Ferndown, in Dorset, were opened for play by the members of the golf club formed there two years previously. Sadly, most of the members were suddenly called away to war and the course was left to decay over the next six years.

Reclamation began again in 1920 under Sir Henry Webb and the success of his work is testified by several descriptions of Ferndown as one of the best parkland courses in England. The course has regularly hosted some of the top amateur tournaments in Britain and several on the European circuit, including the Hennessy Cognac Cup – a national team event – in 1982 and 1984, the European Ladies Championship in 1988 and the British Ladies Open in 1989.

Percy Alliss was the professional for over a quarter of a century. Taking over from Percy in 1967 was Doug Sewell, no stranger himself to tournament play, having won the English

---

Ferndown

- **If you have a small green with a large area of 'fairway' just in front of it, consider hitting that large area safely rather than gambling on the green**
- **On a long putt keep the body and head very still, rocking the shoulders and arms freely in a tightly held 'triangle'**
- **Don't play trick shots. Keep it simple!**

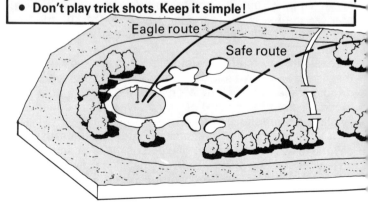

Looking towards the green of the 5th hole at Ferndown, which is one of the best parkland courses in England. The gap in the trees (arrowed) is the aiming point to find the centre of the green.

Amateur Strokeplay and the English Amateur Championship – both twice; having been joint winner of the 1970 Martini Classic, level with Peter Thompson; and having been a member of the British team for the Eisenhower Trophy in 1960 when he played against 19-year-old Jack Nicklaus.

"He hit the ball 200 yards past everyone else!" Doug recalled of the young man who was to become one of golf's legends.

Doug Sewell also played regularly in the mini-Ryder Cup, an event still held annually between club professionals on both

Although a 3-wood to the green is tempting, there is a possible loss of control with distance and direction. It is wiser to play safe and to land on the far side of the stream.

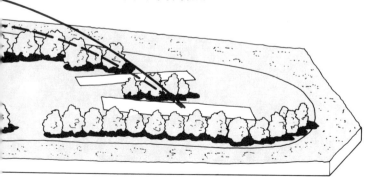

sides of the Atlantic, and was five times chosen for the England team in the Home Internationals.

He does, therefore, know something about the game of golf!

This much experience was too much to pass by, so it was with a sense of awe yet keen anticipation that I arrived at Ferndown Golf Club one glorious Spring-like afternoon to seek his guidance on playing the par-3 5th.

There are, first of all, two tees, separated by a line of trees, the championship tee, which we used, being to the left and further back, making the hole a 208 yard challenge; the medal tee is on the right at 176 yards.

Four bunkers – two either side – protect the front of the green; a row of trees lines the back of the green. There is a stream which crosses the 'fairway' 50 yards from the front of the green. Should you fail to clear that (140 yards from the back tee – 110 from the medal), you would still have a shot but the ground is similar to semi-rough.

We played, naturally, from the championship tee.

"When you look towards the green you can see a gap in the trees at the back, and through it the ladies' tee for the 6th," Doug Sewell suggested. "Aim for that and the ball will find the centre of the green, keeping the shot safely away from the bunkers either side at the front of the green."

It is, of course, always good to have a definite target in mind, even though you may not wish to go as far as that target.

Looking back from the green. A 3-iron, teed up, should finish on the large area in front of the green (arrowed). As the average player receives a stroke, net par is straightforward from there.

"The stroke index on the hole is nine, so the majority of players here will gain a stroke, giving them a four for a net par. With the pin set at 210 yards today and slightly right, so that it is protected by the bunker, a shot of that distance for a middle handicapper could be difficult. If you hit a 3-wood, or for some a driver, the ball will keep on rolling and you will, in any case, lose some control over the direction and length, particularly with the wind swirling around as it is today."

That wind was also quite strongly against us.

"Look carefully at what there is *before* the green. While a good player, with little wind, could hit a wood to the green, the average player would be better off looking at that vast expanse of ground – all of it safe – just the other side of that stream. To be safe the shot from here is about 145 yards, and the bunkers come into play at 196 yards.

"You have, therefore, an area 50 yards long and probably 60 yards or more wide as your target, just 150 yards away. Doesn't that really sound easier than trying to hit a 10 by 10 yard target at 210 yards?"

I had to agree, even though the common ("I can hit the green on a par-3") approach will tempt many of us to ignore this sensible advice.

Without really having to prove the point we stood aside and watched four four-balls play through, playing from the medal tee. Of the sixteen only three hit the green – and all of them were single-figure handicappers. If you stand and watch any par-3 at any club you might be surprised at how few actually do hit the green.

"For an average player I would suggest a teed-up 3-iron hit to that large area in front of the green would be ideal. By not aiming for extra distance to hit the green, and thus being slightly more relaxed, you will probably hit a better shot anyway.

"Land as centrally as you can and then you are left with just a little chip-and-run up to the pin, from 30 or 40 yards. For that, use a 7-iron and just push it up like a putting stroke. Unless you do anything really drastically wrong you will be on the green in position for two putts to get down for your net par."

We then moved on to the green itself, having hit the two shots as directed, making the hole much easier than having to worry about getting a big shot onto the green.

Here we were left with a putt of about 30 feet. Doug stressed how important it is to keep the putter-head moving through the ball on putts of this length.

"Too many players come into the ball and then stop. What is happening is that they are slowing down before they reach the

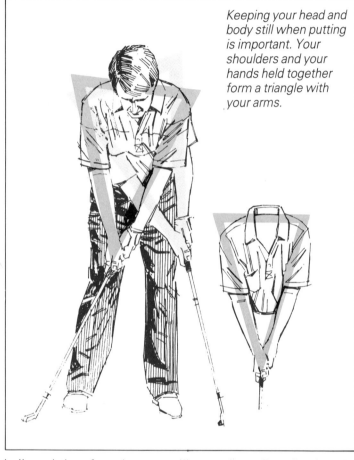

Keeping your head and body still when putting is important. Your shoulders and your hands held together form a triangle with your arms.

ball, and therefore the putt will stay short. By adjusting the weight of your swing, but keeping the putter coming through the ball, you will give it extra topspin and distance, getting it closer to the pin. Make sure you follow through, keep going through that ball!

"When you are putting it is important to remember to keep your head and body still. Stand over the ball, with your eyes above the ball, and really rock your shoulders to-and-fro. Practise it, keep your head perfectly still and just gently rock your shoulders, your hands held together forming a triangle with your arms."

This, then was a lesson in simplicity from a highly experienced player and teacher. And the real lesson is that that is the way to play golf – no trick shots, no lucky bounces.

Yale University, Connecticut, USA
David Paterson, Club Professional

9th hole, 250 yards

In 1701 a collegiate school was established in New Haven, Connecticut. By 1718 its name had been changed to Yale College, in honour of Elihu Yale, a major contributor to the college's upkeep. The college was granted a charter in 1745 and the school, long since renamed Yale University, is one of the major seats of advanced learning in the United States.

Sporting facilities are predictably excellent for the cream of American youth as they study for their degrees. Although a full range of sports is available, of interest to us is the excellent golf course laid out in the hills above the various campuses, a

The spectacular view from the back tee on the 9th hole at Yale University, showing the huge lake from the elevated back tee. The distance to the edge of the green is about 180 yards.

course designed in 1925 by one of the leading American course architects of the time, Seth J Raynor.

The club professional at the course is David Paterson, a native of Scotland who began his professional career under the expert tutelage of Bob Jamieson at Turnberry. After leaving the Scottish coastal course, David spent some time in Bermuda, then played on the US circuit for a couple of years before coming north to Yale.

The course is a testing series of holes, many with narrow fairways where accuracy is vital. Arguably the most testing hole on the course, however, and one which people drive hundreds of miles just to look at, is the par-3 9th, modelled on a hole at Biarritz.

Now with many par-3 holes the green is tiny. Here at Yale that is hardly the case. The green – really a double green – is enormous, covering some half an acre, almost 2,500 square yards. The average par-3 green is about 500 square yards!

There should, therefore, be little problem, you might think, in hitting the green. Yes, well, the course architect was rather more cunning than to give the golfer such an easy target without just a hint of difficulty, and that difficulty manifests itself when you step onto the 9th tee and look down.

The tee is elevated – some 30 yards high – and the distance to

As the green is split in two by the hollow, you need to measure the length of your shot carefully. If you land past the hollow, you will have to negotiate it with your putt.

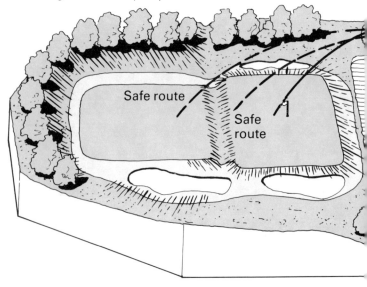

the edge of the green is about 180 yards. To the back of the green the shot measures 250 yards, a full drive and more!

The real problem, David explained to me as we stood there, is 'the lake'! We looked across this vast expanse of water to where I could vaguely make out the distant shore.

"There is another problem," David told me – as if I needed more. The green is split into two with a six-feet chasm in between that is still part of the putting surface.

"You have to very carefully measure the length of the shot – too far and you end up on the back level of the green; too short and the ball is in the water."

The pin today was on the front part of the green.

"If you land the ball in the chasm you have a serious problem. Such a wall, in front of you to putt up, is rare on any course and you need a firm putting stroke with good direction."

The borrow on the green is horrendous, anything up to ten feet is normal!

Yale

- **On a long putt you must make a strong commitment to the follow-through; don't stop halfway through the stroke**
- **Topspin on a long putt – hitting the ball forward in your stance – will keep it rolling and give extra distance**

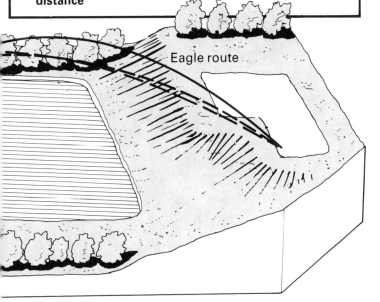

Eagle route

The first problem, though, is to hit a long enough shot to carry the water, and get the ball on the right part of the green. A nervous player should just take a 3-wood and hit high to the green. Getting to the green should really present no problem, unless you are so put off by the thought of hitting over water that you duff the shot completely and ask the ball to take swimming lessons.

Only a few people ever do that of course. A couple of years ago they drained the lake and found 30,000 gently rotting golf balls, together with several golf clubs!

The best tee shot that I could manage was a 4-wood teed up very slightly to eliminate the nerves that I get when I know I have to hit high and long. I aimed for the centre of the green.

The wind is a factor for although the tee and green are sheltered by the surrounding trees it can be quite disturbing to see the ball change direction out over the open water as the wind catches it.

The ball landed on the back part of the green, giving me a shot of over 220 yards with a little draw to add distance. The height off the tee helps, of course. The only problem now was

The enormous green covers an area of nearly 2,500 square yards, about five times the size of an average par-3 green. The six feet hollow and large borrow add to the fun.

With long putts, play the ball at the front of the stance so that you hit the ball on the up, giving it topspin and extra length. Stay still through the stroke and follow-through.

the little putt across the back half of the green, down the slope, up the slope and across to the pin which was near the front of the green!

"Play the ball at the front of the stance," advised David, "to ensure sufficient roll from a topspin action. As you hit it, the putter is coming up, like a driver, and hits the ball with topspin. That gives it more length.

"Make absolutely certain that you remain still during the stroke, but make a much stronger stroke than normal, and more than you think you will need. There has to be a strong commitment to the follow through, extending the arms forward with the putter head still pointing at the target, but don't forget that borrow!"

The majority of players leave themselves short, David told me, by failing to hit the putt hard enough and seeing it roll gently back down into that chasm.

Would I have done something as silly as that!

St Mellion, Cornwall, UK
Tony Moore, Club Professional

11th hole, 203 yards

'The Course that Jack Built' is how the publicity brochures for St Mellion describe the magnificent setting – and course – not far from Plymouth. St Mellion, though, is proud that it is in Cornwall, one of the most beautiful parts of England. Naturally the Jack in question is the great Jack Nicklaus who is not just one of the world's greatest living golfers but also one of the premier modern course architects.

The setting and the facilities are superb, and the Nicklaus Course is as testing as you will find in the world of golf. Its official opening, in July 1988 was an exhibition by the highest quality golfers, when Jack Nicklaus and Tom Watson took on Sandy Lyle and Nick Faldo – almost a mini Ryder Cup match –

St Mellion

- It is not a sign of weakness taking a wood on the tee of a par-3
- If you are hitting an iron off the tee of a par-3, make sure you continue to hit down and through the ball, taking a divot. But always use a tee

---

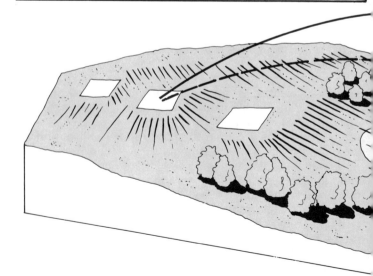

Looking towards the green on the 11th at St Mellion. The tee is elevated about 40 feet above the green and the water represents quite a major hazard.

in an 18-hole exhibition game, played in the most atrocious weather. Despite Jack's intimate knowledge of the course, Faldo and Lyle emerged the winners – wet, but victorious.

The course, seen on a clear, sunny day, certainly is beautiful and very difficult. Tony Moore, the club professional, is one of the best teachers in the south-west of England, and chose for

The water hazard gets bigger the closer you move to the green. From the back tee, at 203 yards, the water is only just visible. St Mellion is an extremely testing course.

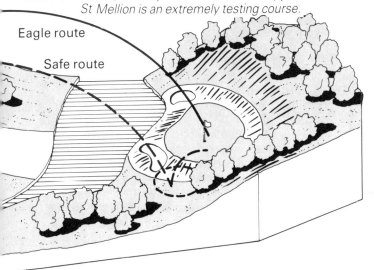

Eagle route

Safe route

The wind is normally against you so you need to use more club than you might at first think. A 4-iron or a 5-wood are perhaps the best choice to carry the 181 yards.

our lesson the par-3 11th, a difficult 203 yard tee shot over water that is barely visible from the tee.

The tee is very elevated, perhaps 40 feet or more in height above the green. And the water is a fairly substantial hazard that gets bigger the closer you move to the green. From the back tee, playing the hole as the pros did, at 203 yards, the water is only just visible and hardly a distraction for the golfer who sees only the green.

Not everybody plays it from the back, of course, most visiting amateur golfers preferring to use the middle tee at 181 yards. With an elevated tee this should, in principle, make it a fairly straightforward shot, hit high in the right direction.

That, of course, is in principle. Unfortunately for most of us, reality is rather different. Tony Moore explained the best strategy for the hole.

"If you discard the idea of hitting the water, the hole is far more difficult than it appears. The wind is normally against you so the shot has to be hit with a little more club than you think."

For the distance we were playing – the 181 yards – and with the green well below the level of the tee, I would be looking to hit a 4-iron or perhaps a 5-wood. But which club is the best choice, if they both hit the same distance? Tony Moore gave me the answer.

"I suggest a 5-wood, because you will hit it higher and be more confident in the shot. Many players tend to dig a 4-iron into the ground, not really connecting with the ball and subsequently hitting it short, often into the water.

"With an iron you hit down on the ball. With a wood, you sweep it away, hitting it up. For most players that means far more confidence in the shot, because the club gets the ball up and they don't have to worry about hitting it high."

We stood on the tee and watched two groups play through. Of the eight only two hit the green. Six used irons, two used 5-woods. Guess which players were using the woods?

"On this hole you must get the distance right, and the only

Tony Moore, Club Professional at St Mellion. On most par-3 tees you will see few divot marks but at a pro tournament the opposite is true. With a teed-up iron you must hit down on the ball.

safe way to do that is to use the wood," Tony emphasized. "It gives you distance and helps you make a smoother swing, because you are not having to think about hitting the ball up. You just sweep it away and the club does the work. With a 5-wood – or perhaps a 4- if you have one – the shaft is shorter than on a driver for example, so you are closer to the ball and can have better control.

"Too many players dislike taking a wood on a short par-3. They feel that it is somehow, weakness to have to hit a wood. Yet we are looking at a distance of about 190 yards to hit the back of the green. Many golfers struggle for that on a drive!

"Ignore what your pals take. Play sensible golf. Hit a 3-, 4- or 5-wood depending on the wind and your own distance. Aim at the right side of the green, the shortest route with the way the water comes in, and just swing smoothly, sweeping the ball off the tee."

A very slight draw on the shot would be ideal here – yet anyone going left with a fade will risk not carrying the water, so the draw or straight shot to the right side of the green is safer.

Tony explained why many of us struggle to get the ball up with an iron, off the tee at a short hole.

"If you look at the ground here on this, or any other par-3 tee you will see very few divot marks. Go to a pro tournament, watch them on a par-3 and see the number of divots left on the tee at the end of the day. Club golfers think that, because they tee the ball – as they should on every par-3 – they have to hit the ball *up* off that tee as they do with a wood.

"That is not the case. With an iron, if you hit *down* the ball goes *up*! It is one of those strange facts of nature which players have a problem understanding. So, if they use an iron off a tee-peg they try to hit it *up*. All that does, with anything stronger than a 5-iron, is hit the ball in a flat trajectory."

The ball still rises, of course, because it is being pushed upwards by the angle that the club-face comes into the ball.

"The difference, however," Tony continued, "is that if you hit *down* with an iron into the back of the ball, it will rise, travel farther and sit down when it hits the green.

"Tee the ball low, just above the ground, and have the ball about the middle of your stance. Then, as you hit down on the ball as you would on any other long iron shot, continue through the ball, taking a divot just as you would from the fairway. All you are doing with the tee-peg is giving yourself the best possible lie."

I mentioned to Tony that, at pro tournaments when I have been watching good golfers play from par-3 tees, I heard a dull 'thud' as the club takes the divot after it has hit the ball. Yet very few of we club golfers do this, preferring to take the ball off 'clean' from the tee-peg.

"When you are hitting an iron from a tee, don't adopt quite the same stance as you would for a wood. With a wood your left shoulder at address is slightly higher, helping you to come through under the ball and sweep it off the tee. With an iron you are flatter at the shoulders, which should bring you down into the back of the ball and on through the divot.

"Don't be afraid of taking a divot off the tee if you are using an iron."

Hitting a teed iron shot. The ball should be teed low and be in the middle of your stance. If you hit down, the ball will rise, travel further and sit down when it hits the green.

Royal County Down, N. Ireland
Ernie Jones, Club Professional

4th hole, 217 yards

The Mountains of Mourne stand silently guarding the small town of Newcastle on the east coast of Ireland, in County Down, some thirty miles south of Belfast. On the natural sand dunes that line the shores of the Irish Sea here, an outstanding golf course has been created. It is the home of the Royal County Down Golf Club, one of the best and most beautiful links golf courses in the world.

The Royal County Down Golf Club, which celebrated its centenary in 1989, has, at its members' disposal, one of the best and most beautiful links golf courses in the world.

The professional here for the past twenty years is Ernie Jones who, as a player, won the Kenya Open in 1971, the PGA Cup in 1976 and played in the Canada Cup of 1965. A past Captain of the Irish PGA, he is the Vice-Captain of the PGA in 1991, a post which normally leads to the Captaincy the following year, the highest honour that his fellow-professionals can bestow on any of their peers.

His playing days are far from over, however, continuing long after he finished the regular Tours in 1972; he won the Irish

---

Royal County Down

- **Concentrate on hitting a shot – not on *hitting the ball***
- **Don't let the hole intimidate you. You have to *dominate* the hole**

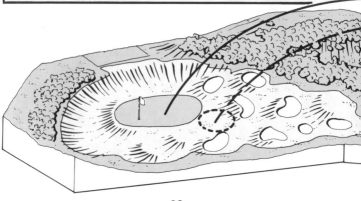

The romantic scenery around Royal County Down, one of the most beautiful links courses in the world. This is the view from the tee of the 4th hole looking towards the green.

Open Seniors in 1984 and the PGA Seniors in 1986. He is also an honorary member of the US Seniors Tour.

From this you will have deduced that he can hit a ball!

And that is exactly what he did the morning we went out onto the 217 yard 4th on the course, a daunting shot across the whin-bushes (gorse) that were in full flower, forming a sea of dark yellow between us and the green.

His shot, with a 2-iron off a tee just showing above the ground, started off in that low, gently rising trajectory that only

The bushes look intimidating but to reach the safety of the front of the green a shot of only some 180 yards is needed. If you are worried at missing the green you have to go left.

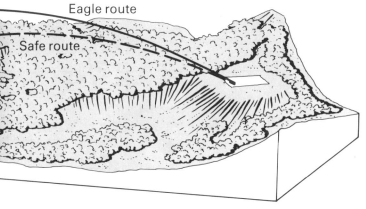

Eagle route

Safe route

professionals can hit, turning slightly left in mid-air as it neared the green, before landing ten feet short of the pin.

He then handed me the club: "Your turn now."

But first he gave me some friendly advice.

"The first thing to do when on the tee is to concentrate on hitting a *shot* – not think about hitting the *ball*.

"Too many players," he explained, "just think about hitting the ball. What you ought to be thinking about is where you want the ball, how high you want it, whether you want it to turn left or right, and what distance you want it. That is the major difference between amateurs and professionals – the amateurs think about the ball, the professionals think about the shot.

"The bushes here look more intimidating than they really are. All you need to carry them to the safety of the front of the green is a shot of just about 180 yards – surely manageable from the elevated tee."

The front of the green itself is 203 yards off the tee, so a good high shot with a little draw would be perfect. As Ernie had just hit that one I didn't really think I could improve on it.

Without a full follow-through it is simply not possible to get the full distance on your shots. Here is the position for a 2-iron hit 200 yards.

"This hole tests the mind more than the golf," Ernie contended, a point with which I would agree. Although the bushes certainly appear to be a major factor on this hole, they are not. Round the green are no fewer than ten bunkers, most of them deep and virtually invisible from the tee, merging, as they do, with the surrounding sand dunes.

"If you do feel uncomfortable about missing the green, you have to go left," Ernie stated. "That is the only place to miss the green. Go right and you are out of the game; go short and you risk either the whin-bushes or one of the bunkers. The shot too long will roll through the green and down a bank, but it is rare to carry the green completely – it is, after all, 240 yards from the tee."

I decided to go slightly left and landed the ball safely 180 yards, four yards short of one of the bunkers, leaving me with a pitch to the pin 40 yards away, good enough, with an accurate

My approach shot of 40 yards was from just in front of one of the bunkers. There are no less than ten bunkers surrounding the green and few of them are visible from the tee.

Looking back from the green towards the tee. It is important with a hole like this, argues Club Professional Ernie Jones, not to allow it to intimidate you.

pitch, to get a three, or at the most a four. With an index of fifteen the accurate pitch in was needed.

One of the differences in our tee shots was that Ernie's 2-iron had left a divot. Mine didn't.

"When you hit an iron from a very low tee, giving yourself a good lie, you must still try to hit *down* on the ball, as you should from the fairway. Too many golfers try to hit it up, yet golf is a game of opposites. Hit down and the ball will go up. You must get to the bottom of the ball as you hit it, coming back to the address position. Don't forget it."

With those glorious mountains in the background this tee shot is one you could happily play all day, a point which Ernie was quick to take up.

"The hole is a test of your nerves as much as your skill. If you could play this hole eighteen times a day for a whole week, by the time you went away you'd be some player.

"You must not let the hole play or intimidate you. It is a hole you have to *play*!"

Turnberry, Scotland
Bob Jamieson, Club Professional

15th hole, 168 yards

Jim Buchanan (Kennemer), David Paterson (Yale), Renton Doig (St Pierre), Gregor Jamieson (Lake Nona), all professionals from whom I have been fortunate enough to have a lesson, have one thing in common. They began their professional careers at Turnberry under the expert guidance of one of the leading golf teachers in the world, Bob Jamieson.

Many other golf professionals learnt their trade at the windswept course on the Ayrshire coast, Bob's fatherly care sending them on their way equipped with the teaching skills that are evident from their contributions to this series of books. It was, therefore, something of a pilgrimage to the small pro shop by the first tee of the famous Ailsa Course to meet him.

In what he described as a 'fine drizzle', fine enough to have prompted Noah to have nipped down to the local boatyard to order the Ark, we set out to the most testing par-3 on the famous course.

The view at Turnberry on a clear day is incomparable: the distant hills of the Mull of Kintyre, the far distant coast of Northern Ireland, and dominating everything, the cottage-loaf shape of the Ailsa Craig rising silently, mysteriously, out of the

The beautiful Ailsa Course at Turnberry on the west coast of Scotland is ranked among the top ten golf courses in the British Isles. This is the view from the tee of the 15th hole.

In the foreground, arrowed, is the deep ravine which makes it imperative to hit the centre of the green. The wind coming in off the sea into your face adds to the difficulty.

cold deep waters of the North Channel separating Scotland from Ireland.

It is difficult to imagine that in the war years Turnberry was a Bomber Command airfield, crisscrossed by roads and runways, parts of which still run across the course, overgrown reminders of sadder times. Turnberry today, however, is a magnificent course, good enough to hold the Open, last here in 1986 when Greg Norman was the champion.

The four par-3s on this course are marked as the easiest – the stroke indices coming in at 15, 16, 17 and 18, a rare occurrence in golf, but one that we have been lucky enough to come across twice in this book. Do not be deceived, however, for the 15th at

The name of the hole – 'Ga Canny' – should be heeded. You can play safe by aiming left for the patch of rough before you reach the green or you can go long beyond the flag.

Turnberry is not easy. 'Ga Canny' – 'go easy' – is the name of the hole, which is in a magnificent setting, the rock of Ailsa rising out of the sea to our right, and the famous lighthouse behind us.

There are two distinct tees, one for the champions, one for us. While the professionals have to hit 209 yards to the centre of the green, we have a shot of 168 yards, but no less difficult. To the left of the green are three bunkers and then rough; to the right and running along the line of the shot from the tee to the back of the green, is a deep ravine, some thirty feet below us.

"The only shot here," Bob Jamieson announced, "is to the centre of the green. You just can't afford to miss it."

It really is a test of good golf, particularly if you are brave enough to play it off the back tee. The wind, coming in off the sea to our right and normally into our faces, is a major factor, prompting Bob to show me the correct way of hitting a long ball into the wind.

"Many people think that if you hit it high it will bite immediately it hits the green. On a long shot this is not the case, because the ball will not come down vertically."

On a short, pitch or bunker shot this might be different where you are playing for position not length.

"As the ball, hit high, begins to get held back by the wind, it stops spinning backwards. As it bounces it will continue to roll

Turnberry

- Many golfers are scared of hitting the back of the green, yet that is the safest and softest part – nobody ever goes there!
- Err on the long side on a putt, Never up, never in!
- Hitting into the wind it is best to keep the ball low. To do this swing in a flatter plane, not as upright as you might normally

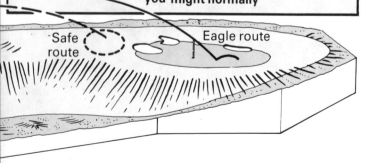

Safe route

Eagle route

on, making it difficult for you to control its distance. A ball hit lower into the wind will maintain its backspin, and will bite more when it lands.

"To do that, and with the wind today, we are looking at perhaps a 4-wood for the average player. Tee the ball a little higher than usual, have it slightly forward in your stance and swing through it with a flatter arc than normal, so that you are coming through it on the upswing. This will keep it lower, putting enough topspin on it to carry the distance.

"To keep the ball lower into the wind - thereby reducing the distance the wind pushes it around – the swing needs to be flatter; that is the club swings round the body in a flatter plane. It is sometimes referred to as not such an upright swing, but

To get a long ball hit high into the wind to bite on landing, tee the ball higher than usual, slightly forward in your stance, and swing through with a flatter arc than normal.

WIND

The greens at Turnberry are quite fast like many links courses, so it is a good idea to err on the longer side with your putting. In the distance are the waters of the North Channel.

you must note that it is the club, not the body that is not so upright. The body is in its normal position, but the club does not get as high above the head as normal, but swings out further round the body.

"If you really feel intimidated by the hole, and have doubts about reaching the green, play safe by taking a 5-iron and aiming left, for the patch of rough before you reach the green. That will still give you a reasonable shot and a possible four, which is far better than missing the green on the right."

Any ball off-line to the right will leave you a very difficult shot back up that hill.

"One thing you could do is to go long, beyond the flag," said Bob, "but obviously not that far as to go right off the back of the green.

"Golfers are scared of the back of the green," he continued, "yet it is the softest part of the green – nobody's ever there! – and will hold the ball better. The front of the green, where everybody walks on, is firmer so the ball will bounce more."

The greens at Turnberry, like most links courses, are fairly fast, but you should never lag a putt up.

"Never up, never in!" Bob emphasized. "Err on the longer side – that way you will make more putts than if you are short."

With a stroke index of 16, this hole needs to be hit in three by many golfers yet Bob has a final word of advice for players who go out on any course.

"Don't worry too much about the par numbers – play the stroke index!"

Sawgrass, Ponte Vedra, Florida, USA

Larry Collins, Head Professional

17th hole, 121 yards

The first par-3 hole on which I took advice is one of the most intimidating, spectacular and most photographed in the world of golf. Ironically, however playing the hole was slightly less daunting than the photographs suggested: proof perhaps that this great game of ours is much more of a thinking person's game than we sometimes assume.

Sawgrass is the headquarters of TPC (Tournament Players' Club), a few miles south of Jacksonville, northern Florida, not far from the Atlantic coast. Sawgrass is, in fact, not just one

Those who hit into the water on the 17th hole at Sawgrass, do not attempt to retrieve their ball as the lake contains alligators. Club selection is the key to playing this hole.

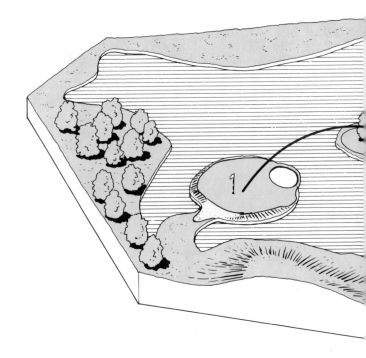

course but five in a magnificent resort setting with a luxurious Marriott hotel, and many villas which are available for rent, at prices that are not as high as you might expect.

The main course is the famous Stadium Course with its notorious and remarkable 17th hole – an island set in the middle of an alligator-infested lake. Balls lost are not retrieved! The lake has never been drained so the number of balls gently rotting is unknown but stand there any day and you can count a couple of hundred trying to swim to the green. One unfortunate but persistent gentleman from New York, who was determined to hit the green if nothing else, actually took 128 shots (almost half of them penalty strokes) before he holed out – quite a bagful of balls to use up on one hole!

Sawgrass

- **Don't try to hit spectacular shots – play safe**
- **Ignore hazards like water – just imagine it's a lovely, wide, green fairway**
- **Play the nine-out-of-ten shot – not the one-out-of-ten!**

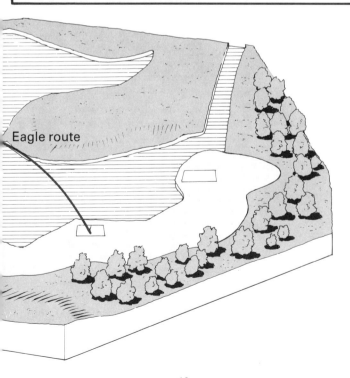

Eagle route

I was fortunate enough to be under the tuition of the Head Professional at TPC, Larry Collins, whose first words to me were reassuring. "It really is no more difficult than hitting the green on any other short par-3 – that is, as long as you ignore the water.

I gazed at him blankly, then across the water at the green, trying to imagine the flight of the ball from the tee to land in the middle of the green, hopefully close to the pin. They say you should visualize shots – but visualization is the easy part!

"Most average golfers look at the water and give themselves a problem," continued Larry Collins. "Normally they would have no difficulty hitting the green, but here they look at the water and virtually persuade themselves they will never hit it.

"Club selection is vital – the key to success on any tight hole, and here even more so. The aim is to take the club for the distance, say an 8-iron for the 120 yards here and add one. So in this case go down to a 7-iron.

"Tee the ball a little higher than you would usually for a short iron, so that you swing normally and clip the ball from well

This is perhaps the most initimidating par-3 in the world but as Larry Collins explains, the problem is mainly in the mind. Most golfers would normally have no problem with this length shot.

underneath, giving it extra height. This automatically gives the ball more back-spin, making it stop faster without running on. By using one club more, you can also afford to grip down – placing your hands a little down the shaft rather than right at the top – which again gives more control on the direction.

"Setting up straight is vital. Your body should be lined up perfectly for the aiming spot, which must be the middle of the green. Forget the pin placement; go for the middle of the green. This gives you more room for error."

He demonstrated how to line the body up, which is often a problem for we average handicap players. The club face is the first thing to align, aiming the base of the blade at right angles to the centre of the green, as with a putter. Then check that your grip is correct. Getting the body straight can prove difficult, but a good way to do it is to look down at your knees at the address.

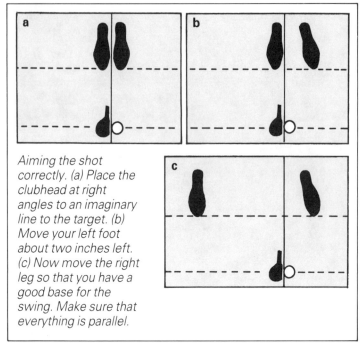

Aiming the shot correctly. (a) Place the clubhead at right angles to an imaginary line to the target. (b) Move your left foot about two inches left. (c) Now move the right leg so that you have a good base for the swing. Make sure that everything is parallel.

You should be able to form a line directly across them to the aiming point."

We tried it. With the tension (it seemed that suddenly several dozen people were keen to watch) my first tee shot, with a 7-iron, landed about 10 feet short of the edge of the green and dived into the water. Not so much of a birdie as a 'gator!

My second shot – third with the penalty stroke – was hit with less tension and, being 'clipped', flew high and straight, and finished about twelve feet from the flag.

Larry explained that a local rule here, allows a player to drop a ball close to the ladies' tee after three have hit the water. That is slightly different from the normal rule for hitting into water as you should drop at the point where the ball crossed the boundary of the hazard. As this is about two feet further forward on this tee, you would be faced with the same shot.

The putt, incidentally, went straight in, giving me a four. As the hole is index two, even with the first shot in the water, that gave me a 'par'.

"The main thing to do here is to play a shot that you are safe with," Larry continued. "Don't try anything spectacular – just aim for the middle of the green. Play the nine-out-of-ten shot, not the one-in-ten!"

Moor Park, Hertfordshire, UK
Ross Whitehead, Club Professional

3rd hole, 165 yards

A thirteenth century mansion used by Henry VIII and Cardinal Wolsey might seem an unusual setting for a golf club. Add the fact that the American 2nd Airborne Division used it as its headquarters during the Second World War and that the raid on Arnhem – as shown in the film ''A Bridge Too Far'' – was planned within its solid granite walls, and the true splendour of the magnificent Moor Park mansion becomes apparent. Indeed, the house now serves as perhaps the most spectacular golf club-house in Britain.

Golf is a very modern addition to the splendours of Moor Park, the game only being introduced there in 1923. Since then, however, it has risen in stature and is now regarded as one of the finest examples of parkland golf in England, hosting the Wang Four Stars competition, an annual pro-am which succeeded the Bob Hope Classic. The Women's Open has also been staged over the course.

The professional here, too, is of the highest reputation, a man who was persuaded to play golf by James Braid, the great golfer and course architect. Ross Whitehead began playing golf in 1947 and turned professional, as an assistant, in 1950. After some time spent under James Braid at Walton Heath, he

Looking towards the green from the tee on the 3rd hole at Moor Park, showing the fine parkland setting of the course. Several important tournaments have been hosted here.

The ring of bunkers surrounding the green requires a carry of at least 135 yards from the tee. From the medal tee a 4- or 5-iron is the club to choose.

went out on the Tour, the normal way ahead for a young man in golf at that time. Ross spent over 20 years competing at the highest level of European golf, coming to Moor Park while still playing in 1965.

He still plays some Senior Tour events and, like many other top teaching professionals in Europe, is looking forward to an expansion of the Seniors Tour on this side of the Atlantic, for nothing beats the thrill of playing golf in a highly competitive environment.

The hole that he chose for us to play was the 165 yards 3rd, a hole that, from the back of the medal tee looks a relatively easy

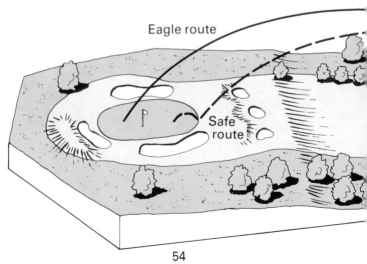

and straightforward challenge. From the championship tee, at 191 yards, it is a different proposition altogether.

The distance to the centre of the green from the medal tee is not that daunting to most players, being about a 5-iron or perhaps a 4-, depending on the wind.

''The thing you must do, though,'' Ross advised, ''is to get the ball up in the air.''

The green itself is some 35 yards front-to-back which on its own is three clubs' difference, a fact often overlooked by club golfers who, 'always hit a 5-iron to this par-3.' Pin position can normally vary by two clubs, so you should try to establish, from the tee, exactly where the pin is placed on the day you play it. Most golf clubs tend to favour the centre of the green to make it simpler for their members, but if you have the chance to check, always do so.

''Close to the green the wind can intrude fairly strongly from the left, being funnelled in. You can't feel it on the tee so you tend to miss it, but a look at the flag might show you that down on the green the wind is blowing. Professionals train them-

It is important on this and many par-3s to check the position of the pin, which can vary on different days by two clubs. It is best to tee to the right and hit slightly across the hole.

Moor Park

- **Although there may be no wind when you are on the tee, check the flag to see if there is any wind on the green**
- **Read the greens *from the tee*, on a par 3**

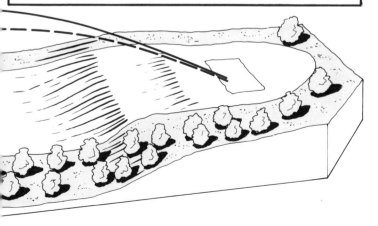

selves to look for these things and to take them into account. The shrewd amateur does too."

Ross suggested that we should also take the trouble to 'read the greens', *from the tee*. "Here, for example, if you look carefully, you can see that the green slopes from left to right. So a ball is likely to roll that way after it lands. It also makes a difference to the putt. As you want to avoid putting downhill if possible, you should be looking to have the ball finish below the hole. On this green that is to the right.

"On this hole be looking to tee on the right, so that you are hitting across the hole, giving yourself more room to aim at. Never be afraid of hitting *across* the hole.

"The ideal club here for most players is probably a 4-iron, depending on their strength," Ross continued. "A 5-wood, too, might help because it gets the ball up higher due to its effective ball-striking loft. A normal 3-iron, for example, has a loft of about 22°. Again, a 5-wood does not have much more at about 24°. However, the face of a 5-wood is further in front of the shaft so it adds about another 6° of effective loft, making it 30°."

In front of the green – and you can only see this from the front of the tee – is a row of three bunkers and a dip. To clear these from the back tee you need a shot of at least 135 yards carry.

"You must hit a high shot to a par-3 green," says Ross, "because a low, running shot will do just that – run off the back of the green! It is uncontrollable. A high shot, on the other

Ross Whitehead, Club Professional at Moor Park, recommends reading the greens from the tee. He also suggests experimenting by taking one club more from the tee on a par-3.

INCORRECT

CORRECT

A common cause for a slice or a pull left is falling back on the right foot during the swing. The swing is then from out-to-in. Keep the line of the body throughout the swing.

hand, will just sit down faster as it lands, giving you more control over its length.

"Do make sure that you hit down on the ball (with an iron) off the tee, taking a divot – which on the tee you do *not* replace.

"You must also always be looking to go over the flag if possible. The vast majority of club golfers land short of the pin, afraid that if they take one club more they will go through the green. Yet most greens are about 30 yards long. That's three clubs in length. Take an extra club next time you're on a par-3. I bet you won't go through the green."

While we are all anxious to improve our shot-making technique and our swings, Ross gave a tip that will put us on a par with the top professionals as we stand on the tee.

"Even without hitting a shot you can improve your golf, just by *reading* the green in front of you. Train yourself to do it!"

Ullna, Sweden

John Cockin, Club Professional

5th hole, 184 yards

The course at Ullna, a dozen miles north of Stockholm, the Swedish capital, is rightly regarded as one of the most beautiful in Scandinavia. For three years in the mid-1980s, it was the venue for the Scandinavian Open, a European Tour event that has now moved to nearby Drottningholm, primarily due to lack of sufficient car-parking space at Ullna for the thousands of spectators.

Ironically, perhaps, the course is now in better shape than ever it was during the tournament's stay here, and a new, enlightened management ably assisted by the professional, John Cockin – himself an ex-European Tour professional – has greatly improved the facilities and benefits to members, both corporate and individual.

The course itself is a virtual loop around a large lake. Forests of pine, birch and oak line the shores, and impinge onto the course at regular intervals, which sometimes makes for interesting shots. Yet dominating the course, and coming into play on several holes, is the lake itself, the home of several dozen species of migrating birds. Year-round regulars include a family of swans that stay close to the shore by the course, and are almost regarded as the club's 'pets'.

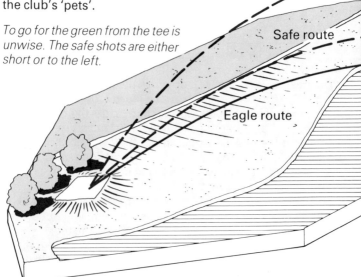

To go for the green from the tee is unwise. The safe shots are either short or to the left.

Safe route

Eagle route

Ullna is one of the loveliest courses in the whole of Scandinavia and loops around a large lake, fringed with forests. This is the view from the tee of the 5th hole.

Ullna

- **Leave a long iron out of your bag and add a 7-wood**

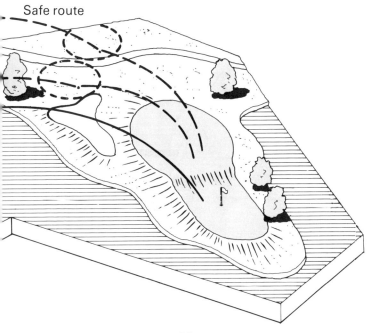

Safe route

On the day of my visit they had positioned themselves in an inlet between the tee and green of the short 5th. This was the hole John Cockin chose for his lesson on par-3 strategy.

The 5th is a difficult hole (unlike two of the other par-3s which require a shot to a water-surrounded green) but it does present golfers with several options, depending on their talent, bravery or good sense.

From the members' tee, very slightly elevated, the green is on an isthmus, sloping left to right towards the lake, part of which, resplendent with swans, juts in front of the green. A full 170 metre (184 yard) carry is essential if you are going to aim for the pin, the last 90 metres (97 yards) of which are across the lake itself.

However there are, as John Cockin pointed out, several other possibilities to consider.

"When you stand on the tee and look at the green, you must take into account your level of golfing ability and skill," John told me. "Any shot aimed directly at the pin today" – placed well to the right making the direct shot the longest carry over the water – "is going to end up a ninety per cent chance of success rate

"That is an unacceptable risk to take – a waste of shots, and of golf balls because most of them will end up in the lake. What you need to do is to look for what options the course designer has given you.

"The direct shot is very difficult for the average golfer. You can't go right and draw a ball in towards the green because that

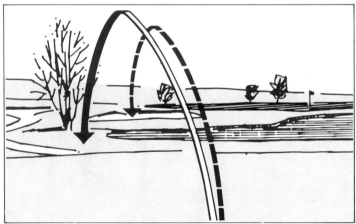

The failure rate in reaching the green directly is high. A short shot to the left leaves a straight second shot to the pin, but the perfect shot could be just short of the bunker.

Looking back from the green across the lake towards the tee, showing the carry of 90 metres (97 yards) across the water.

shot is all over water as well. This leaves you with either a short shot, or a shot to the left."

Every golfer, of course, likes to have a go at the green on a par-3 but here is a hole where that is not good sense. John raised another point to think about.

"The stroke index on this hole is eleven, so ninety five per cent of club golfers gain a stroke. Why not use it and play the hole as a short par-4? Your chances of success are much higher than if you attempt it as a par-3."

On the left side of the green is a large but not deep bunker. Left of that is a tree, and left of that is some semi-rough just over a cart path.

"The perfect shot could be at the bunker," John explained. "With the tendency for most people to slice a little, the ball could just turn prior to landing and hit the upper part of the green, providing the shot is long enough. If it is short, it will hit some semi-rough and leave a chip onto the green.

"Even going further left is good because the ground beyond the path is easy and you would have a straight shot to the pin with nothing in your way."

We then examined what would be needed for each option – discounting that direct-at-the-pin shot, which with a strong wind against us, would have been difficult to control.

"As you want to hit left, stand on the right side of the tee, and give yourself more space to aim at," John recommended. "I would suggest a 3-wood into the wind today but it would vary according to the wind strength and direction. I have hit 6-irons off this tee fairly regularly but I always tell club golfers to try for longer than they think – almost everybody hits short! Aim at

Looking out across the lake from the green on the 5th hole at Ullna. The course has hosted the Swedish Open several times.

the tree on the left but don't think about trying to fade the ball – just hit it straight."

My shot, however, once again found the bunker leaving me a shot to the pin of about 30 metres – a fairly long bunker shot. John explained how to play this.

"This is not like the explosion shot which you would have if the bunker was close to the hole, nor is it a fairway bunker. The first thing to remember is that you *don't* need a sand wedge. Go in with a pitching wedge or even 9-iron and try to play a little chip shot, making sure you take the ball out clean, any sand coming out as a 'divot' after you have hit the ball. You do not need to get the ball very high, as the bunker face is shallow.

"Do not take a big swipe at the ball as if this was a fairway bunker – just play a gentle chip shot aimed directly at the target. Remember that the ball will break once it hits the green, so study the slopes on the green first. Adopt a very slightly open stance to help the hands come through.

"If you land in the semi-rough left you have a similar type of shot, again a chip, though here I would use a 7-iron to keep the ball low and get it onto the green before it bounces. Then it should run all the way to the hole."

One club that is still not as popular in Europe as it should be is the 7-wood.

"A wonderfully versatile club," John enthused. "It gets the ball airborne quickly and is far more controllable than many other clubs, particularly for the middle to high handicapper. It will give more distance than a 4-iron, for example, and give you much more control over your shots in distance and direction. I highly recommend it to every golfer; leave one of your long irons out of the bag and add the 7-wood. It will pay you dividends every time you play."

Noordwijkse Golf Club, Holland
Tom O'Mahoney, Club Professional

17th hole, 175 yards

We have at last discovered a golf hole with three different stroke indices. The first, the official club index for the championship tee, which measures the hole at 186 metres, is fourteen. The medal tee, normally played by the members and visitors, at 161 metres, is twelve. Yet during the KLM Dutch Open when it was held here in 1985, the hole, from that 186 metre tee, proved the sixth most difficult on the course. The course itself, a wonderful true links course separated from the North Sea only by sand dunes, is reputedly the best course in the Netherlands.

We, however, have to stick with the club's official stroke index – from the 161 metre (175 yard) tee – of twelve, giving most of us a stroke, which we need.

Tom O'Mahoney, not a Dutch name, to be sure, has been the club professional here since 1970, though hailing originally from Cork. Tom's original and direct teaching methods are recognised as perhaps the best in Holland, just one of the reasons why he is coach to the Dutch National Team.

"This is a very difficult hole," he told me as we discussed the strategy, "because there is nothing between the tee and the

From the tee the flight towards the green looks fairly easy, but you must hit over the final ridge to have a playable second shot to the green.

63

Looking back from the hill behind the green shows just how difficult the terrain is, should you fail to clear that ridge.

On the 17th at Noordwijk, the only place to miss the green is in front and slightly to the right, where you have the chance to chip up. Go left and you find trouble.

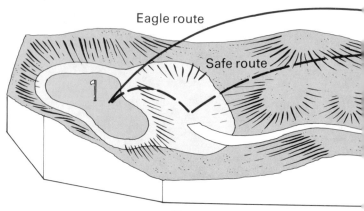

Eagle route

Safe route

green. You have to hit firm and straight, to clear a ridge 20 metres or so in front of the green before you are safe. If you clear that ridge you will have a run-up to the green."

To carry that ridge and reach safety you need a shot of 139 metres (151 yards) which should be within the range of most golfers with a middle or long iron. From the back tee most professionals would be looking at something like a 3-iron to hit the ball high to the back of the green.

"I would suggest a 3- or 4-wood for most golfers," said Tom, "aiming for the rear, right hand side of the green, where the pin normally is and where the green is largest and safest. Although you might be able to clear the ridge fairly easily with a middle iron, to hit the green you will need a wood. From the ridge to the back of the green is a difference of four clubs, two of them on the green itself."

The left side of the green is very narrow and difficult to hit and the right-to-left wind will push the ball further left into trouble. The only safe part of the green is on the right.

"If the pin is towards the front, the back-to-front slope of the green could make a putt back fairly difficult, so an average player is better using the extra stroke that the hole gives you. Hit over the ridge to safety before chipping up to the pin."

That certainly is the safe way to play the hole, though of course many players will be tempted to go for the green. A factor in making a decision is that this is the 17th hole. The decision could easily depend on the state of play, either against an opponent, or against the course. Only you can decide

Noordwijkse

- On chip-and-run shots remember the three 'T's – tracks, triangle and target
- On every shot have a swing-thought

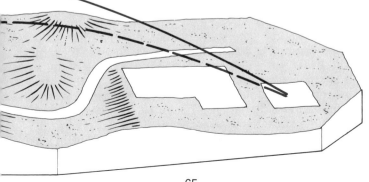

If you miss the green 'safely' at the front right, you then have the opportunity to control a chip up to the green. But don't leave your ball short.

whether you need to play safe with a definite four or to gamble everything on hitting the green and getting down in three or even two. Most professionals win by mixing playing safe with the occasional carefully considered chance.

"One of the problems with just clearing the ridge is that you then have a run up the hill to the green. Too many people leave these shots short by trying to get the ball just this side of the pin. What you should do is aim to go past the flag, playing to the big part of the green.

"On chip-and-run shots I teach the three 'T's – *tracks, triangle, target*. The *tracks* are the lines leading to the target – not necessarily the pin. The *triangle* is the shape of the arms and shoulders, which remain fairly fixed in relation to one another during this stroke. It is reminiscent of a putting stroke – and the *target* is the target. The aim is to swing the *triangle* through the *tracks* to the *target*.

"The weight here is about sixty to seventy per cent on the left side, hands ahead of the ball, ball back in your stance. Keep that triangle fixed and swing back and through to the same level, as on a clock where you go from 7 o'clock to 5 o'clock, or 8 o'clock to 4 o'clock."

This is on an upright clock, not the swing plane clock face, and relates to *this type of shot only*!

"What you must have on every shot," Tom continued, "is a swing-thought. By this I mean a routine; for this shot, a chip and run, not too tight on the grip, correct weight distribution, about 60/40 right, stay close to the ground on the takeaway. That is enough to think about before you line it up. Then just go for the target."

Which is exactly what we did.

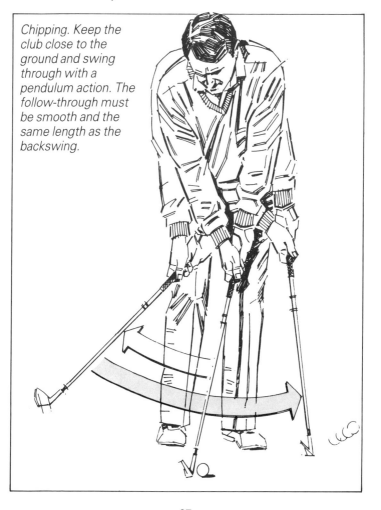

Chipping. Keep the club close to the ground and swing through with a pendulum action. The follow-through must be smooth and the same length as the backswing.

Royal Sydney, Australia
Charles Pettit, Club Professional

14th hole, 194 yards

It was Queen Victoria who granted the Royal Charter to the Sydney Golf Club allowing the club to use the 'Royal' prefix. In 1894 the club moved to its present site at the aptly-named Rose Bay, just outside Sydney. The club professional today is Charles Pettit, who spent several years on the European Tour and is thus an accomplished player and an excellent teacher.

He chose for our lesson the teasing par-3 14th, a hole with two distinct tees, an upper, championship tee at 194 yards, and a lower, members' tee at 186 yards. We played from the upper tee, which is, as its name implies, slightly more elevated and to the left of the lower tee, being separated by trees.

"As you can see the green is very well protected by bunkers," Charles told me as we stood in the hot afternoon Sydney sunshine. We wore hats, which are essential to guard against the burning sun 'down-under'.

"Club selection is vital on a par-3 and it is important to know where the pin is. Too many people ignore that and just play the hole the same length every day."

Royal Sydney

- When out on the course look at the greens of neighbouring holes as you are passing and note the pin positions
- Balata balls achieve better results around the green than Surlyn balls

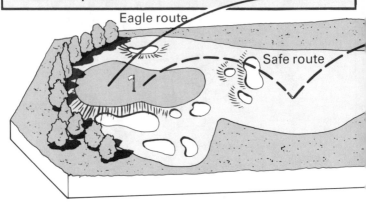

The map shows clearly where to place the tee shot. Use the stroke index cleverly, and if in any doubt, place the tee shot short. Then all you have is a simple chip for a safe four.

Here at Royal Sydney, the green, although fairly narrow, is a massive 46 yards from front to back, potentially changing the length of the hole quite dramatically. Choosing a club to hit the front of the green, some 163 yards from the tee is totally different from choosing a club to hit the back, at 210 yards. For me, for example, that is the difference between a 6-iron and a 3-wood – very different clubs!

"The direction and strength of the wind is also an item for careful consideration," Charles continued, "as again you could end up with a difference of two or three clubs for the same shot in different wind conditions."

The wind today was just a gentle breeze in our favour. Having walked past the green earlier on our way to the tee we had

The short 14th has a very well-protected green and a long shot is needed. Here the higher handicapper, or the player who wants be safe, should stay short of the trouble and aim for a four.

noted that the pin was cut fairly centrally, slightly to the left side of the green. A good tip, when you are on the course, is to look at the greens as you are passing, then when you get round to them you will know the pin position and be able to plan the hole much better.

With the wind and pin position it was ideal to hit a high shot with a hint of draw, but more or less straight.

However, before we did, Charles had some more advice on strategy for the hole.

"Because of the length of this hole the average golfer must play it sensibly. When the wind is strong and against you, it would be very difficult to hit the green *safely* and I would suggest that you take a 5- or 6-iron and lay the ball up before the bunkers in front of the green. Then all you have left is a pitch

over the bunkers to the flag, getting as close as you can, playing the hole as a short par-4. With the stroke index, most players receive a stroke anyway, so that is the sensible way to play it."

And let's be honest, it's the number of strokes in a game of golf that counts, not how far you hit the ball!

Charles also made the point about going for the pin.

"I would always favour the right side of the green here," he told me. "The bunkers on the left are dangerous – the one on the right is a little easier and is greenside, so you could just nip the ball out without too much difficulty. If you are in one of the bunkers on the left, you know you are in a bunker!"

The treacherous, quite deep and steeply banked bunkers on the left slope towards the green, making it difficult to get under the ball. To give you a real idea of why Charles favours the

Charles Pettit demonstrates how to get out of a bunker and keep the ball short. (Left) Take a steep backswing, coming down hard but smooth. Keep the left arm and wrist fixed firm throughout. (Below) The club-face must be open and finish with the back of the left hand, and the blade, pointing skywards.

right-hand side of the green as being the safest, there are six bunkers on the left, one on the right!

"If you are on the green, just look to two-putt, unless you have landed within a few feet of the pin and can safely hole out. If you are on the green but not close, play a defensive putt, just lagging the ball up close to the pin, within a couple of feet."

Our shot today was a 3-iron to carry the distance and stay on line, but I watched as my ball strayed left and fell into one of the dreaded bunkers.

Charles advised me on the best course of action.

"This bunker is fairly deep and you have a high lip to get over. To get out and land very softly fairly close to the hole – within ten yards or so – you need to have a very steep backswing and really punch down to get the ball out high. The takeaway must be really steep, much steeper than normal so that you can come down hard – not snatched, smooth but firm.

"Then in your follow-through keep your left arm straight, restricting the amount of follow-through, but a full shoulder turn will help you turn towards the target. Your feet however, stay firmly anchored.

"It is in the wrists for this type of shot. That steep backswing and downswing are vital, but the follow-through needs very careful examination. After you have hit the ball, with the club-face laid really open and the ball forward in your stance, you keep your wrists locked so as to bring the club-face pointing up in the air. This means the back of your left hand is pointing up to the sky, the back of the right hand down towards the sand. You should bring the club out of the sand in the open position, with some sand sitting on the clubface. That's the test."

To my surprise and satisfaction, my bunker escape shot landed reasonably close – about eight yards – from the pin, and left me a possible chance of a par.

Charles is one of the many professionals who advocate a balata ball – if you can afford them.

"The old, wound balls used to be ideal because they had some feel around the green. Modern players like to think they get extra distance with surlyn balls, but if they used the balata balls they would achieve better results around the green and probably end up with lower scores anyway. Surlyn balls do not split as much and give very slightly better distance off the tee, but only if you hit them perfectly."

On a par-3 you do have to hit a middle to long iron, and stop it on the target so a balata ball is better. If you miss, you have to be delicate. And that, as Charles Pettit so rightly points out, is known as the scoring zone.

Chantilly, France

Patrice Leglise, Professional

6th hole, 215 yards

An hour's drive from Paris, not far from Charles de Gaulle airport, in the middle of a huge forest, is the wonderful town of Chantilly. Chantilly is most famous for its chateau, one of the finest examples of 17th century architecture in France. The aristocracy, before the Revolution, used to come out to Chantilly to stay, getting away from the bustle of Paris.

Nowadays, residents of Paris, or her visitors, can easily get out to Chantilly for the day, enjoying not only some of the best golf in this part of France, but also a memorable meal in one of the many fine restaurants in Chantilly itself or one of the villages in the surrounding forests.

Whatever the level of your golfing ability, a visit to this course, home of the Peugeot French Open, will be a reward in itself. The course is set in beautiful wooded surroundings and

Looking from the tee at Chantilly. You have to carry the first bunker (left), but although the ball will come in off the bank on the right, the safest shot is left.

features some fine holes which will test the best golfers. You will need written permission to play beforehand, however.

Patrice Leglise is one of the professionals here at Chantilly, an accomplished player who, besides teaching, still competes in several tour events a year. He chose for us the testing 14th, possibly the most difficult of the four short holes on the course, rated as handicap twelve, even though the 198 metre (214 yards) 6th is rated seven.

The championship tee – not in use the day of our visit, as it was being prepared for the forthcoming French Open – measures an impressive 199 metres (215 yards). We used the members' tee, at 180 metres (195 yards).

The tee is elevated considerably above the level of the green, which gave me the feeling that I had some control over the

(Below) Even a driver, hit low with inevitable fade, will work here because there is room on the left for the ball to run round.

Chantilly

- Correct club selection is vital on a par-3
- The most important part of golf is played over just six inches – the six inches between the ears!
- Think *well*!
- Most sport is dynamic, but as golf is 'static' you have to make your mind dynamic

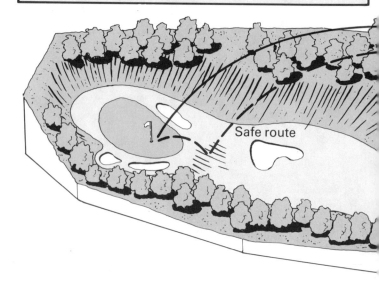

The view from the green looking back, showing the height of the tee. If you aim to hit the green, you must remember that you need less club than normal. The green also slopes from the front left.

hole. The reality was rather different. The green lies below in a valley, with wooded banks either side. Although the green is fairly long, some 42 metres (45 yards) front to back, it slopes from the front left to the back right – normally the way that the ball rolls.

Although the day of my visit was very hot, climbing to over 30°C, there was a gentle breeze. On this hole the breeze comes up from the green to the tee, funnelled up by the banks on either side. The hole, therefore, plays longer than it appears.

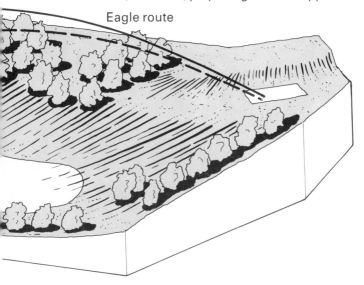

Eagle route

From the tee, the land drops away sharply to the 'valley' floor – the flatter area of grass which is labelled 'fairway' only starting some 80 metres (87 yards) from the front of the green. There is, therefore, a carry of 120 metres (130 yards) minimum required to get the ball into position. Downhill, that should present no problem for any golfer.

Protecting the green, as with most par-3s, are bunkers, two left and two right. More ominously there is a large bunker 40 metres (43 yards) short of the green in the centre of the 'fairway'.

"To score well on this hole," Patrice told me, "you must at least carry that bunker.

"Club selection is important. From the back tee a tour pro, like Faldo, would take perhaps a 4-iron. A club professional, like me, would use a 3-iron. The club golfer will need a 3-wood or even a driver.

"There is, however, only one way to play the hole," he continued. "The right hand side is not safe – only the left. Therefore aim slightly left and allow the ball to fade right.

"A strong player should tee up a 3-wood land and the ball beyond that large bunker, near to the front of the green, with the club and body very slightly open, aiming a little left of the

From just behind the large, first bunker. The run to the green from here is trouble-free, so it is a safe shot if you feel you won't hit the grass.

bunker. That should bring the ball round as it lands, and slow it down. Once it hits the green it will start rolling right."

You must be careful, however, in aiming left, that you do not go too far, or hook the ball, otherwise the ball will be difficult to find let alone play.

If the ball does roll off the back of the green, or bounces off right of the green (not before it) you will have a chance to chip it back, for the valley-like layout will stop the ball going too far. It is also easier to putt back uphill than down.

"The weaker player, who has some difficulty landing the ball on the front of the green, can play it short quite safely, again if he stays left of that bunker and perhaps even short of it," Patrice continued. "For him a 5-wood might be good, and if he lands short he will have either a strong wedge or a weak 9-iron to the green, keeping the ball low; in some cases just running it onto the green if the approach is flat."

The most interesting shot though, to this green, was perhaps unorthodox yet highly effective, particularly for the higher handicap golfer.

"This type of golfer, or perhaps a lady or senior player whose distance is not too good, would be advised to take the driver, tee the ball normally, and hit it straight to the left of that bunker without trying to over-hit it. The ball will fade almost every time and will bounce and run, landing on the green."

Strange but true. Because the shot is downhill, there is no pressure on the higher handicapper to get the ball airborne, and the lack of loft on the driver face will put topspin on the ball, making it roll and roll.

The one thing to avoid at all costs on this hole is a draw. That would only make it bounce off the left hand edge of the green – or miss it altogether – probably ending either in one of the bunkers on the left or in the trees.

"The most important part of playing this hole," Patrice concluded, "or of any other hole, is concentration.

"Sport is dynamic, that is fast moving. Golf, on the other hand, is played from a static ball position and your initial position at address is perfectly still. The body, then, being static, has to be balanced by a dynamic mind – that is a mind which can visualize the swing, the ball flying through the air and landing where you want it.

"To do this you need powerful concentration, but in a positive manner; it's no good worrying about missing the green, or landing in a bunker. You have to think positively, concentrating your mind on the place either on the green or on the fairway where you *want* your ball to land. Think well!"

Baltusrol, Springfield, New Jersey, USA

Bob Ross, Professional

4th hole, 194 yards

Imagine having to play a shot 194 yards – the last 80 yards or so across water – to a pocket handerchief-sized green that slopes towards the water. The green has three deep bunkers at the back and then a hill. If you do land on the hill, you are faced with a downhill chip to a green where the ball moves like lightning. If you are too short you land in the lake and you can't go left or right because there are trees everywhere.

In short, a nice, easy par-3!

That's the shot we faced on the fourth hole at Baltusrol Golf Club, Springfield, New Jersey. Bob Ross, who won both the Philadelphia Open and Pennsylvania Open in 1987 and now plays some events on the Senior Tour, saw my look of horror as he stood watching me gaze across to the miniscule green.

"All the trouble is in front, here," he cheerfully told me. "There is *no* bail-out on this hole, you *have* to hit the green!"

Didn't I know it!

Bob reminded me that Tom Watson aced this hole during the 1980 US Open, when the players use a forward tee at just 162 yards on the first two days of the Open, it being considered too

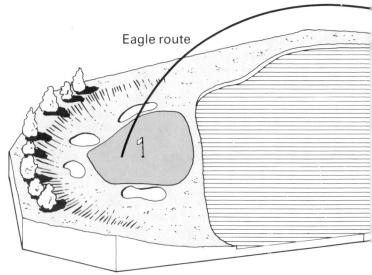

Eagle route

The view from the green of the 4th at Baltusrol, showing the imposing club-house in the distance.

difficult for all of them to hit from the back tee! The Open is back here in 1993 so you can see it is a top course. There was also the time when the great Robert Trent Jones, having been asked by the club to redesign the hole as it was proving too difficult for the members, was playing it with the President of the PGA.

"Nothing difficult about this hole!" Robert Trent Jones exclaimed after he had aced it! To us mere mortals, though, the hole is fraught with danger. Yet all you need to do is carry the lake, stay out of the bunkers and keep off that hill behind the green! Simple, isn't it?

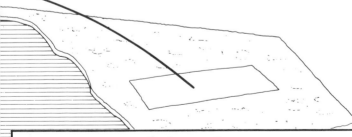

Baltusrol

- A ball loses distance if you hit it high off a tee so you should compensate by taking extra club
- Low shots won't work on many par-3s as they will often skip over the green. High shots are usually needed

There really is no alternative on this shot – no 'bail-out' area. The shot from the green must be very high and also very long. Don't forget the wind factor.

Mr Trent Jones teed up, swung, and sent the ball across the lake straight into the hole.

"Nothing difficult about that!" he muttered, marching off round the lake to pick his ball out of the hole.

When the pin is on the right of the green the hole plays even longer because of the angle of the green to the lake; if left or centre it plays just very slightly easier, perhaps one club less than on the right.

"The best shot here," Bob told me, "is very high because you want it to come down and bite fast. A long iron, always hit off a tee, will be best, so take the club with which you normally hit 195 yards and go directly for the centre of the green. It must be a high shot – a low shot just won't work because it will skip off the green the second it lands, leaving you with a very difficult downhill chip that will cost you dearly."

"Does a ball lose distance as you hit it higher off a tee?" I asked Bob.

"Yes, it does," he replied, "so you should compensate by taking extra club. Here the wind coming at you from the hill and across the lake will catch the ball and push it down onto the green. You must, therefore, carry the water. Don't be short!"

If you do go through into the rough or sand traps behind the green the difficulty is stopping the ball as it comes out, the green running downhill away from you, and very fast.

"It has to be a very delicate shot," Bob told me. "You must stand very open and hit with a lot of cut – the club coming out-to-in across the ball – with a much faster release. The right hand comes through and flicks the ball up with backspin.

"It has to be very delicate, very soft – but if it's too soft you risk leaving the ball in the sand.

"The other vital point to think about is to place that bunker shot. The green slopes so immediately the ball lands it will begin rolling downhill.

"What you have to do is choose the place you want it – and can reasonably expect to get it – then work back, calculating how it will roll and where you should aim to land it. You must read the break on the green into that bunker shot.

"Of course you might not be able to get it safely close to the pin out of the sand. If you can't, then work out how you can best get back to a safe position without wasting shots. Aim for the safest part of the green open to you."

A very tricky hole, designed to test your nerves as well as your accuracy with a long iron!

For a delicate shot back to a downhill green, stand very open and come round the ball, out-to-in, using a fast hand release. Vary the length of the backswing, exaggerated here to show the direction of the club path.

Royal Melbourne, Australia
Bruce Green, Club Professional

7th hole, 146 yards

Many of Australia's top golf tournaments are held on the testing Royal Melbourne course. The championship course itself, however, is a composite of holes from the two magnificent courses – East and West – at the beautiful setting just outside the capital of Victoria.

My visit to Royal Melbourne took place during the 1990 Coca-Cola Classic, a A$700,000 tournament which featured players of the stature of Rodger Davis, Peter Fowler, Craig Stadler and the eventual winner, Ronan Rafferty.

On the final day Rafferty was in the last group out on course. As he passed the par-3 7th (which is also the 7th on the West course) the club's professional, Bruce Green and I were

(Below) "Club selection is vital on par-3s," says Bruce Green. Here is another hole with no 'bail-out' area, but you must aim for the left side of the green.

Royal Melbourne

- On the tee of a par-4 you have a big target, perhaps 50 yards wide. With a par-3 you have a target maybe 10 yards across
- Club selection is the most vital point of hitting a par-3

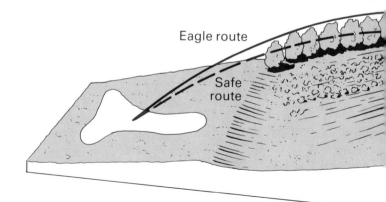

Eagle route

Safe route

During the tournament, the pin was directly behind the bunkers, drawing the shots right and into trouble. Ignore the pin and aim for the biggest part of the green that you can see.

waiting, clubs at the ready, to play the same hole. Immediately the 'big boys' had played through and had cleared the green heading for the 8th tee, Bruce and I set ourselves up on the 7th tee. This was to the bewilderment of a group of spectators who thought that Rafferty's group, as leaders at the start of the day, were the last group through. Having over a hundred spectators is something else, I can assure you.

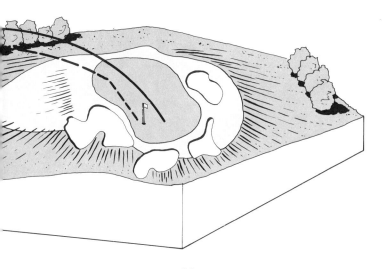

"Many club players get on a par-3 thinking it is easy," Bruce began. "But in fact par-3s are the most difficult holes on a golf course. You see far more bogeys, even in a professional golf tournament, than on other holes.

"The distance may be shorter but par-3 greens are notoriously difficult to hit. The greens are often smaller. They are normally well bunkered and if you miss them the surrounding area is treacherous, with the greens often being elevated, so you always have to pitch uphill if you miss them.

"Check the scorecard for the stroke index on most courses and you will find the par-3s amongst the most difficult.

Once Rafferty and his group had cleared the green it was time for Bruce Green and myself. Here Bruce hits his 7-iron to the safe side of the green.

"The other major problem on a par-3 is that you have to hit a very accurate shot from 'cold'. On the approach to a par-4 or par-5 green you have already hit one or two shots and so are 'warm'. Then you cool down by putting and walk to the tee of a three where you have to hit the target, first time!

"On the tee of a par-4 you have a big target – maybe 50 yards wide. When you get to the tee of a par-3 you have a target maybe 10 yards across."

It surprised me that I had not thought of this before.

"You need," Bruce continued, "a little more preparation than normal if you want to hit the green on a par-3. Quite often you see players move onto the tee before marking their cards from the previous hole. That is quite wrong.

"Move off the previous green, of course, but stop before you get to the tee and mark your score. Never replay that missed putt from three feet. Of course you'll hole it the second time."

The 7th hole here is a very steep, uphill shot, 135 metres (146 yards) to the centre of the green, which slopes back-left-to-right-front. The right and the back of the green then drop away some 30 feet, so, as Bruce says, if you miss it you are in deep trouble. A huge bunker guards the front right side of the green. As the pin was directly behind that bunker to the right of the green, the only part of the green that was visible from the tee was the left.

"Correct club selection is the most vital point of hitting a par-3," Bruce told me. "It is, of course, essential that you know how far you hit each club, but take into account the fact that this is uphill and that you want to get the ball higher and drop it down on the green softly rather than hitting a low, running type of shot. Also, don't forget the wind.

"However, you do have two advantages on a par-3," Bruce said. "You can tee the ball – *always do so* – and you can choose the place from which you want to hit the shot, within reason.

"You have the width of the tee to choose from, so take the spot that will give you the best line into the area of green that you want to hit.

"Aim as close as you can to the middle of the green, but stay away from that bunker on the right. If you hit the centre of the green you will have a putt of maybe 20 feet. Hit the edge of the green and that could be 60 feet!"

Bruce took a 7-iron and sent the ball flying up to land on the green; I took a 6-iron. Normally I would hit a 6-iron about 150 yards but today I was 'cold', despite the 89°F temperature. I also had an audience and had to hit uphill high, which loses distance. I teed the ball up on the left of the teeing area, higher than Rafferty had five minutes earlier. I took the half dozen

A long putt awaits you once you reach the green. If you hit the centre the distance will be 20 feet, and from the edge the distance could be 60 feet.

practice swings that Bruce Green recommends on a par-3 tee, checked my alignment and . . . we made it!

As a polite round of applause from our dwindling audience died away, I started off towards the green before Bruce reminded me that I had left the bag of clubs behind! So I had to swallow my pride and go back and shoulder the bag up the hill.

"One of the reasons for having those few practice swings," Bruce continued as we lugged our way uphill for two putts for par, "is that you have come to the tee 'cold'. You need to get the swing rhythm going again, naturally without having to think about anything other than alignment. I have seen too many people trying to figure out what's wrong with their game halfway through a round.

"You can't do it there. *Paralysis by analysis* is really the biggest threat to your game out on the course. Get your professional to help you if there is something wrong. When you are out on the course, *just hit it*!"

San Remo, Italy
Mauro Bianco, Club Professional

9th hole, 210 yards

Some of the par-3s in this book are fairly long, needing, in some cases, a wood off the tee. I recall one par-3 at Waterville in Ireland where the big-hitting Liam Higgins, and I both needed a driver to reach the green, some 210 yards away. Mind you, there was quite a wind blowing!

However, some par-3s live up to their name as the 'short holes', though in my experience they are never as easy as they look on paper. Such a hole was the one chosen by the professional at San Remo, in the south west of Italy, on the Mediterranean coast not far from the border with France.

San Remo is a lively town built in a small, sheltered valley between gigantic folds of the massive Alpes Maritimes which roll down from distant Switzerland. Today the town has grown considerably, with so much pressure on space that half the inhabitants now live in buildings clinging to the mountain side. This has not discouraged them from growing the most glorious flowers, famous throughout Italy, in glass-houses which, like

Very short, but extremely tricky, the 9th at San Remo requires little more than a sand wedge. You can't run the ball in but you must hit, and stay on, the green.

the homes of the growers, are perched on every little ridge available, catching the almost constant sunshine.

The golf course, too, shares the local characteristics, being both mountainous and compact. Although it measures 5,203 metres (nearly 5,700 yards), and is confined to an area less than half that which many other courses enjoy, it never seems crowded or claustrophobic. It runs up and down the mountain-side, each fairway cut off from its neighbours by trees, or perched on the mountain ridge above.

It is a test of fitness though, and I would not recommend it to anyone who is unfit or who would be discouraged by some pretty steep climbs.

The 9th hole is at the highest point of the course, as well as being furthest from the club-house, and it was a good walk getting up there. It nestles virtually under the autostrada that runs from the French border to Genoa, part of the vast 2,000

Missing the green is not an option in this case and would be very costly. Accuracy and length are absolutely vital on what should be an easy enough hole.

San Remo

- **On a short shot you have a more upright swing than with a driver**
- **Concentrate on swinging, not on hitting the ball**
- **When you're close to the green, don't think about fading or drawing the ball – just aim for the flag**

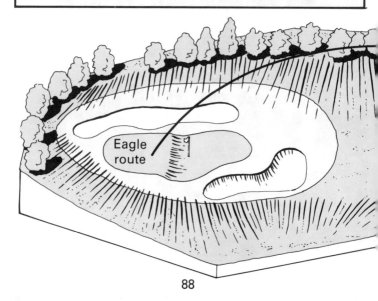

Mauro Bianco, a respected teacher and tournament player.

kilometre (1,250 mile) motorway from Alicante in southern Spain to Reggio, on the toe of Italy.

Our host on the course was the club professional and European Tour player Mauro Bianco, a young man who, only born in 1962, has gained a wealth of experience in this great game, which he started playing at the age of five. He has been the professional here since 1984.

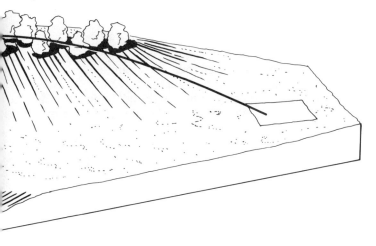

You cannot go right, because the ball will bounce off the side hill, or land in the bunker. A recovery shot which would hold on the green would then be difficult.

"This hole is the shortest on the course, with a stroke index of 17, but you must treat it with respect.

"Although it is short you need an accurate tee shot because the green is small. In front there are bunkers guarding the approach, so you can't run the ball up."

The view from the tee is inland, looking at the mountains but part of the hillside obscures the right side of the green, forcing you to consider playing left.

"Playing left," Mauro warned, "is something you must *not* do. If you miss the green left or too long your ball will probably roll a couple of hundred feet down the mountain."

Par might then be rather difficult!

"Tee the ball, even on a hole this short," Mauro advised. "It gives you a good lie and with a shot like this you want to get the ball high to land softly on the green. With this kind of shot when you want to hit high, you need to sweep it off the tee, rather than hitting down and taking a divot. Here, a wedge or 9-iron will be enough club but sweep under it, clipping the bottom of the ball. This is, remember, a very short shot."

The technique for this type of shot means that you should stand more open.

"About 20 degrees open," suggested Mauro, "with the ball in the middle of your stance. Try to swing the same with every club rather than having a different swing with every club – be consistent.''

There is, however, one small difference on this type of shot as Mauro explained.

''The swing is more upright and you are standing closer to the ball. With a longer iron the ball is further away and you turn more on the backswing in a longer, flatter arc. With this one the swing is more upright, so the club moves on a straighter plane through the ball – not such a pronounced in-to-on target-to-in sequence as with some other clubs.''

The green is two-tier, the higher level being at the back, so a professional like Mauro would go for the back and bring the ball back down, if the pin is on the front tier. He would use a sand wedge. With the type of ball most club golfers use, and their inability to create good backspin, their aim should be at the *top* of the flag using a pitching wedge.

The green is very small, only 20 metres long and 15 wide so accuracy is vital.

''Keep the club face square to the target,'' Mauro insisted, ''and aim straight. Don't think about drawing or fading the ball in on this shot. Just hit it straight. Aim for the flag – be brave!''

The open stance helps promote a better follow-through, providing the club face is pointing at the flag. With an open

You cannot go left, or too long, or you face this very difficult shot back up the steep hill to the green, where once again you will have trouble controlling the ball.

With the shorter shots you stand more over the ball, with an upright swing. With longer irons, however, you are further from the ball, so swing flatter and get more clubhead speed.

stance you are, in fact, hitting a slight fade, but don't do it deliberately. If you set up the body and club correctly – body slightly open, club at the target – it will happen.

"Why do some people miss-hit this type of shot?" I asked.

"Two reasons," Mauro responded. "They either look up too quickly to see the effect of their shot; or they have too much weight on the right foot and they then don't transfer their weight correctly.

"You must also have a good body turn – swing is important. Too many players worry about the ball, but if they concentrated on the swing they would hit ninety per cent good shots.

"Hit the swing – not the ball!"

La Herreria GC, Spain
The Final Hole

13th hole, 196 yards

Having travelled the seven seas – or most of them – in pursuit of our series of par-3 holes, from Scotland's January gales on the Ayrshire coast at Turnberry, to San Remo in Italian sunshine; from the sophisticated surroundings of Chantilly in France to Ullna, far north in Sweden; then from Europe across the Atlantic to the United States and on round the other side of the globe to Sydney and Melbourne in January for some 'winter' warmth, we come, at last, to that final test – the last hole.

This is where we temporarily discard our teachers – but not their advice – and, for one hole, 'go solo' in the hope that we will prove what we have learned, and will put it to good use.

It's nice to go travelling, but even nicer to come home, so this time I ventured only a short distance, no more than thirty miles from my home in Madrid to the tiny mountain village of San Lorenzo de el Escorial, nestling in the foothills of the majestic Sierra de Guadarrama range which tower above the Spanish capital.

In the shadows of El Escorial's famous and spectacular monastery is La Herreria golf course, a club whose membership of over 3,000 indicates its popularity, though thankfully not all of them are regular weekend players!

The course is beautifully laid out with the holes winding their way through the woods. A stream, swollen in winter but a mere trickle in summer, runs alongside many of the fairways. The mountains and monastery form a magnificent backdrop to this wonderful course where, one July morning, the Director of the club, Luis Crespo, walked out with me to the 13th hole for this end-of-term exam.

The 13th is a fairly straightforward hole, with a superb view of the Escorial and the mountains. It measures 179 metres (196 yards) with a stroke index of 7, so we gain an extra shot here.

The difficulty comes in the shape of shot. The green is not out of reach from the tee, particularly at this height above sea-level (1200 metres, about 4000 feet) – but the best shot is a high one which will come down steeply and land precisely.

The other option is to take a low, long runner that comes in from the left to end on the slightly elevated green.

Bruce Green it was, from Royal Melbourne back in that January sunshine, with the temperature similar to today – 96°F

The final test. From the tee the fairway is straightforward and looks as though you could play safe and short. The view, with the Escorial in the background, is spectacular.

– who advised us to warm up on a par-3. Having just come from the previous green, it is wise to take several practice swings to tone the muscles again, for the tee shot on a par-3 really needs to be accurate.

A second sound procedure, as Ross Whitehead from Moor Park advised us, is to 'read the green from the tee', so that we know where to put our tee shot.

In this case from the tee the green appeared slightly elevated, the approach area sloping left to right with the shape of the mountain. Quite obviously, anything short was going to roll that way. The green itself looked fairly flat, with bunkers left and right, and one at the back to catch anything too long.

The wind needs to be taken into account, as it comes off the mountains from the left. A short tee shot would be safe but not too far right.

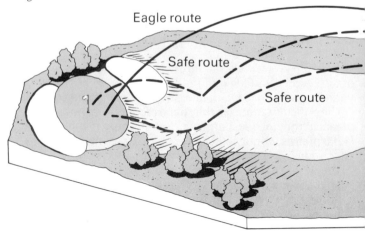

Doug Sewell, at Ferndown, recommended using a large 'bail-out' area on a long par-3 if available. That certainly was an option here, but at this height, and in this heat, you are always one or two clubs better off. Normally a 200 yard shot would mean, for me, a 3-wood or a well-struck 1-iron. Here, a 5-wood or a 3-iron was enough, but if in doubt take a longer club and swing easier. You will still get the distance but be able to hold the control much better.

I chose a graphite 5-wood, hoping to use its height to hit the front of the green and stop. The ball was teed fairly low, just above the ground, giving it the perfect lie so essential on tee shots. When using an iron off the tee, it is vital to remember to follow through and down, taking a divot. With a wood you can't do that as you need to sweep the ball off the tee cleanly.

One important point that has been made is to ensure that you are lined up correctly, to where you want the· ball to go. It is essential to have the back of the left hand pointing towards the target. Personally, I have found this a more precise method of ensuring the grip is correct than the 'V's' formed by the fingers and thumbs.

Having got the alignment and grip right, the shot needs to be firm and smooth. The backswing must be high enough back to cock the wrists, thus generating the power. Keeping the head still is a well-known 'commandment' but I still try to concentrate on this during the couple of practice swings before I step up to the ball.

The follow-through is also vital, as Nick Brunyard from Krefeld emphasized.

"On the follow-through, after you have hit the ball, try to cast the club head directly at the target," he said. This helps extend the right arm more, something you should feel if you are hitting

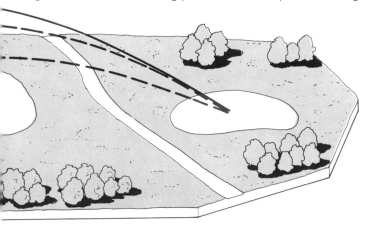

Par-3s need to be treated with respect and must be carefully planned. Sometimes playing short and safe is the sensible choice, rather than going for the flag every time.

correctly. The wrists, however, must 'release', the right rolling over the left – not *under* it!

The ball flew well in the bright sky. I had aimed for the left side of the green and put a little draw on the ball to hold it straight – the breeze coming down off the mountain pushes the ball right. The breeze also pushes the ball down (as it had at Baltusrol) so the distance is held back a little but the ball will die on landing.

Coming down just short of the green, with the bounce it rolled up onto the slightly elevated green, finishing about thirty feet short of the pin.

Had it been shorter it would have been safe because the approach area is wide with no hazards. That is the answer for anyone who is slightly short off the tee – a long, low running shot is ideal in these conditions.

Two putts, the first aimed at a small mark on the grass close to the hole, the second aimed directly at the back of the hole, saw us safely in for a three – net birdie.

We have learnt how difficult par-3s can be, and how they have to be treated with respect. Choosing the correct club is vital, but if the tee shot looks too difficult, the safety shot, to the 'bail-out' area, is the sensible thing to do. As so many professionals have asked: 'why try something spectacular but difficult when you can do something sensible and safe?'